VERMONT . . . WHO KNEW?

Appreciation of "Vermont...Who Knew?"

Robert Wilson's *Vermont... Who Knew?* is a quirky guide to some of the usual and many of the unusual attractions, history, and characters that make Vermont what it is today.

Think of the book as offering an idiosyncratic tour of Vermont with a chatty, indefatigable guide who has learned a lot about Vermont and is willing to learn more.

The book is organized south-to-north, by region, and after a few state-wide entries , including Vermont's short history as an independent republic ("Vermont was born original," Wilson declares.) — we join the author as he roams through most of the state, selecting unusual events, museums, and individuals to profile, or at least mention.

In southeastern Vermont, for example, he presents the familiar story of Rudyard Kipling's troubled years in Vermont — and a profile of a decidedly unfamiliar Vermonter — Darrell Ward, inventor of the bedpan banjo.

Wilson's choices of items to feature are completely his own, often charming, and sometimes perplexing. He mentions the Hubbardton Battlefield, but skips any mention of the Bennington Battle Monument —possibly because the towering stone obelisk commemorates a battle that actually took place a few miles away in Hoosick Falls, New York. There's a mention of the wonderful Calvin Coolidge Homestead in the tiny village of Plymouth Notch, but not a word about the equally wonderful Marsh-Billings-Rockefeller National Historical Park in nearby Woodstock.

But guidebook inclusiveness is not the point of this author's per-egrinations. His entries are clearly people and places in Vermont that appealed to him, and several of his most appealing choices are individuals that the average tourist would miss. Sprinkled throughout the book are profiles of colorful local Vermonters. There's Valari Freeborne, who runs an old-fashioned ("Headquarters for Men") barbershop in Springfield, cartoonist Ed Koren in Brookfield, and Patrick Palmer's horse-and-wagon trash service in Bristol, among others.

It's an interesting mix — historic sites and events, a wide variety of museums, personal interviews with local people, and a few plain old good stories. They combine to make this book as entertaining and oddball as the state it surveys.

—Tom Slayton

Few know more about this state and its stories than writer, editor, and radio commentator Tom Slayton. That he took time to read and talk about a few more of them in this book is my privilege and good luck. Thank you, Tom.

VERMONT... WHO KNEW?

QUIRKY CHARACTERS, UNSUNG HEROES, AND WHOLESOME, OFFBEAT STUFF

ROBERT F. WILSON

FOREWORD BY U.S. SENATOR BERNIE SANDERS

PHOTOGRAPHS BY VICTORIA BLEWER

CARTOGRAPHER AND PICTURE EDITOR,
ELIZABETH JAEGER LAWSON

Wilson McLeran, Inc.
Saxtons River, Vermont

The prices, rates, and hours listed in this guidebook were confirmed at press time. We recommend that you also call establishments to obtain current information before traveling.

Photos by Victoria Blewer unless otherwise credited
Interior design by Jetlaunch
Cover design by Debbie O'Byrne
Maps by Betsy Jaeger Lawson

Library of Congress Cataloging-in-Publication Data is available on file.

ISBN 978-0-943837-03-1

Printed in the United States of America

10   9   8   7   6   5   4   3   2

For Bart, Zootie, and Gene;
those they held close: Sue, Joan, and Toss;
and their totems: Da Bearss and Basie

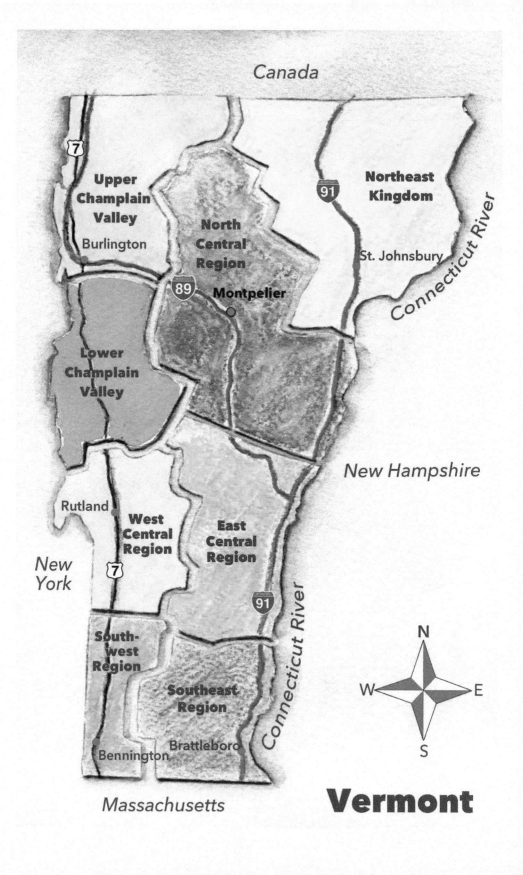

CONTENTS

Acknowledgments viii

Foreword by Bernie Sanders, U.S. Senator x

Preface xii

Prologue xiv

Chapter 1: Statewide 1

Chapter 2: Southeast 25

Chapter 3: Southwest 65

Chapter 4: East Central 83

Chapter 5: West Central 115

Chapter 6: North Central 135

Chapter 7: Lower Champlain Valley 163

Chapter 8: Northeast Kingdom 177

Chapter 9: Upper Champlain Valley 201

Bibliography 229

Appendix 231

Index 236

About the Author 241

About the Cartographer and Photo Editor 241

About the Photographer 241

ACKNOWLEDGMENTS

Many Vermonters, as well as a few former residents, have contributed to the content of this book. Suggestions came in welcome and diverse ways.

Several kind experts in Vermont history or sociology include David Deen, former state representative and steward, Connecticut River Watershed Council; Richard Ewald, Former Rockingham development director; and Richard Stickney.

A number of knowledgeable individuals have contributed information or source material for specific entries. Among them were Eloise Beil, Lake Champlain Maritime Museum; Allan Berggren, M.D.; Jan Cannon, CEO, Jan Cannon Films; Kins Collins; Meg Dansereau, Graton Associates, Inc.; Elizabeth Davis, Boardman and Davis Communications; Vincent DiBernardo, DVM; Jim Esden, Forester II, Vermont Department of Forests, Parks & Recreation; Jack Galt, facilities director, Flynn Center for the Performing Arts; Arnold Graton, restoration conservationist, Graton Associates, Inc.; Sue Halpern, Scholar-in-Residence, Middlebury College; Jennifer B. Hare; Trish Hanson, Entomologist, Vermont Department of Forests, Parks, and Recreation; Joshua Krugman, Bread & Puppet Theater; Bob Paquin, aide to U.S. senator Patrick Leahy; Sherri Potvin, Executive Director, Lake Champlain Islands Economic Development Association; Barbara Schultz, Forest Health Program Manager, Vermont Department of Forests, Parks & Reccreation; Elka Schumann, Bread & Puppet Theater; Susan Shea, Green Mountain Club; Ken Slater, Vice President, Springfield Telescope Makers; Don and Dave Trachte; Claudio Velez, architect, PLLC; Jack Weaver, D.D.S.; and John Wood, former director and founder of the Master of Fine Arts Program In Creative Writing and Professor Emeritus of Photographic History and English Literature at McNeese State University.

Several creative Vermonters have suggested topics or entries that were included in one or more chapters: Tom MacPhee, former Bellows Falls First Selectman; the late Albert Neill; Warren S. Patrick; Jim Reagan; Cary Romano; Todd Roy; and Scott Wheeler, publisher, *Vermont's Northland Journal.*

The Major L.L.B. Angas story, in chapter 2, was a group effort, pieced together from the remarkable memories of Saxtons River residents Bob Campbell, Averill C. Larsen, David Moore, and the late Albert Neill.

The engraving accompanying the Phineas Gage story in chapter 5 is reprinted from the *American Journal of Medical Sciences,* n.s. v. 20 (July 1850): 13–22 Bigelow, Henry J., "Dr. Harlow's case of recovery from the passage of an iron bar through the head," courtesy of the Harvard Medical Library in the Francis A. Countway Library of Medicine.

Martha Buchanan's research of primary and secondary sources provided much of the raw data that got many entries off the ground; she generated ideas for additional entries and sidebars, as well.

Betsy Jaeger Lawson designed and created the chapter-opener maps and served as picture editor, bird-dogging elusive photos, improving the quality of others with her Photoshop skills, and generally tracking the whereabouts and quality of seventy-plus images.

Photographs by Victoria Blewer, unless otherwise credited. In addition to the numerous photos taken for the book, Victoria contributed several story ideas.

Michele de Filippo, owner of 1106 Design, answered all questions over the nine months the book approached printing readiness.

To those I've neglected to include or have listed erroneously, I apologize. Please bring instances of such stupidity to my attention, and I'll make amends in the next edition.

FOREWORD

Vermont is a state of great natural beauty, of mountains and valleys, of forests and farms, of villages and vibrant small cities. The generosity of Vermont's landscape is matched by the generosity of its people.

Vermont also is a state with a long history, a history filled with innovation. Visitors to our state, as well as Vermont residents, will find *Vermont . . . Who Knew?* full of brief descriptions of Yankee ingenuity, and, since the book is organized geographically and contains plenty of roadside directions, they will learn where to find those examples of ingenuity.

Readers will, in these pages, encounter Vermont's remarkable network of 5,000 miles of snowmobile trails stretching from Canada to Massachusetts, maintained by a volunteer network known as VAST, with its 138 chapters. Readers will briefly meet Justin Morrill, the high school dropout who became a U.S. senator and established the land grant colleges of this country, opening higher education to the children of working-class families. They will find out how to visit King Arthur Flour in Norwich, which today flourishes as a wonderful example of an employee-owned company.

They'll learn about the first ski tow in America, about hang gliding, about Barre's granite quarries, about the world's longest two-span wooden bridge. They'll encounter the birth of "The Free and Independent State of Vermont" in Windsor, a year before the Constitution was ratified.

This book is an informative and pleasurable compendium to those who want to travel Vermont and see things not found in most guidebooks and will be a delight to those who enjoy finding out about "quirky characters, unsung heroes, and wholesome, offbeat stuff."

Bernie Sanders
U.S. Senator

PREFACE

In and around the Arctic Circle, a condition called "permafrost" causes a mixture of underground moisture and soil to freeze into a concrete-like mass—sturdy enough (until recently, anyway) to support highways and three-story buildings, winter and summer, year after year. In Vermont, a bit south and slightly milder, we're lucky enough not to have such a climate. Instead, dozens of microclimates produce a winter moisture and soil combination that freezes much more randomly, causing sharp upthrusts particularly noticeable on secondary roads. Motorists quickly adapt, however, especially when alerted by road signs reading FROST HEAVES AHEAD!

This brings us to Vermont's only professional basketball team: Here's to the Frost Heaves! Any state serious enough of purpose to name an athletic team in honor of indigenous geological phenomena rather than mammals of prey earns points for originality. The team's tag line challenged upcoming opponents by evoking the origins of its name: "We're gonna be the bump in their road." The Frost Heaves were indeed that from 2005 to 2011, winning two national championships in the American Basketball Association, and a cumulative record of 93-22. In the middle of the 2011 season, with a fan base that surprisingly had slipped to fewer than 1,000, the team ceased operations. A half-decade of glory, but their diminished fan base was sad indeed to see them go.

Vermont was *born* original, as you'll see in chapter 1. Pressured by New Hampshire to the east, by New York to the west, and by Massachusetts to the south to give up more and more land back in the 1700s, it declined membership as one of the first thirteen united states, deciding instead to go its own way as a sovereign nation. It finally joined the union as the 14th state in 1791, under more favorable terms.

Fifty years later, Rev. Hosea Beckley noted in *The History of Vermont* that Vermonters "are not ashamed to be seen going to Boston in caps made of their own mountain fur; in striped woolens manufactured within their own dwellings; in vehicles constructed by themselves; and drawn by horses of their own raising." Residents today who come from Vermont families going back six or more generations are known for this same iconoclastic spirit. Newcomers who see something about the state and its people that makes them want to live here too, soon adapt to it. Those who don't adapt usually don't stay. I'm entering only my third decade as a Vermonter, meaning neither I nor my progeny will ever shed the label "Flatlander," adhering to all inhabitants who don't yet have four generations of ancestors "in the ground." My wife, born in Alaska, at least has a face-saving comeback. I grew up in Illinois, where the highest point in my former county is Bald Mound, at 739 feet. Not much I can do about it now.

Vermont . . . Who Knew? is organized geographically, the first chapter dealing with statewide matters—historical, geographical, and cultural. The remaining eight chapters cover regions delineated on the map on page iv. The remarkable people, events, and curiosities represented by on these pages are but a fraction of the total that *could* have been included, limited only by time and space. On the acknowledgments pages you'll see that this was anything but a one-man job. I had all the help I needed. All I had to do was ask.

N.B.: To add an additional sight-and-sound dimension to our coverage, citations following roughly half of the entries lead to one or more YouTube videos, or videos from other sources, credited where possible and referenced specifically to the topics covered. These can be accessed by entering the three- or four-word title (listed just below the applicable entry) into the youtube.com search box. At your destination you may well find additional coverage. Enjoy, as time and interest permit.

Bob Wilson
www.robertfwilson.net / Robertrfwilson@gmail.com

PROLOGUE

An unlucky fellow died one day and wound up in the long line of judgment. As he waited, he noticed that some souls marched through the pearly gates straight into Heaven, while others were led over to Satan, who promptly threw them into the fires of Hell.

Every so often the man saw Satan tossing a poor soul off to one side into a small pile instead of into the fire. Finally, the man's curiosity got the better of him.

"Excuse me, Prince of Darkness," he said. "Why are you tossing some wretches aside, instead of flinging them into the fire with the others?"

"Ah, those," said Satan. "They're from Vermont. They're still too cold and wet to burn."

—Anonymous

1

STATEWIDE

Some of this state's curiosities and oddities stretch across multiple regions. The Long Trail, for example, starts in Massachusetts and scales just about every mountaintop in the way of its zigzag route to Canada. Twenty-one years after its completion, it became the inspiration for (and shared part of its route with) the better-known Appalachian Trail.

You'll want to know more about Champ and Memphré, two pre-historic monsters who dwell in the deeps of two northern and relatively placid bodies of water. That's what some say, anyway; others aren't so sure one way or the other.

Water knows no boundaries, which is why the devastating flood of 1927 story is appropriate in this chapter. Tropical storm Irene, which followed in 2011, was fully as destructive. We recount the experience of a victim who suffered yet happened to be a thousand miles away.

Finally, difficult as this may be to believe, Vermont was a nation before it was a state. Back in the 1600s everybody wanted a piece of this stunning real estate. Massachusetts claimed part of it. So did New York and New Hampshire. But Vermont's leaders declined membership as the fourteenth of the original colonies and decided the state should go its own way as a sovereign nation. You might say it seceded from what wasn't yet even the United States of America. And that's where we begin this curious story.

By the way, If you need a rousing pep talk about climate change, 350.org founder Bill McKibben has written just what you're looking for.

THE SOVEREIGN NATION OF VERMONT

"Vermont" is an English name taken from Les Monts Verts, *which is what French explorer Samuel de Champlain called Vermont's Green Mountains on his 1647 map.*

Quick, name the original thirteen United States. Let's see . . . Massachusetts, Connecticut, Vermont . . . Wrong! Actually, Vermont did not join the union until 1791, as the fourteenth state. In 1777, with Massachusetts, New Hampshire, and New York all trying to swallow up parts of the colony, Vermont thumbed its nose at its neighbors and everyone else and wrote its own constitution as a free and independent republic, answerable to nobody. On July 4 the constitution of Vermont was drafted at Elijah West's tavern in Windsor and adopted by the delegates on July 8 after four days of debate.

All this was due to some double-dealing by King George III. In effect, King George handed over Vermont to both New Hampshire and New York. He granted New Hampshire's governor, John Wentworth, all land to within 30 miles of the Hudson River and then turned around and gave New York the land all the way to the east bank of the Connecticut River. Massachusetts jumped in and claimed some of it, too. Instead of caving in, delegates from 28 towns assembled and declared themselves independent from the jurisdictions and land claims both of the British colony of Quebec and the American states of New Hampshire, New York, and Massachusetts.

Between 1777 and 1791 Vermont governed itself as a sovereign entity, with the town of Windsor as its capital. It convened an elected assembly, created and operated a postal service, coined its own money, and outlawed slavery throughout the state (as the U.S. Constitution of 1787 did not). Thomas Chittenden was its first—and only—president. During this time Vermont's militia, led by Ethan Allen (as general of the army of Vermont) and his Green Mountain Boys successfully beat off attempts by surrounding states to annex parts of the state. In 1778 Allen was captured by the British, taken to New York, and after a few days exchanged for British colonel Archibald Campbell. In 1791 Vermont paid New York $30,000 dollars to settle all its land disputes and was admitted to the Union.

Vermont's dedication to independence has become a distinguishing characteristic. For example, that Vermont became a republic so irritated the State of Georgia that its legislature issued a proclamation saying, in part: "The whole state should be made into an island and towed out to sea." On September 29, 1941, the State of Vermont declared war on Germany—more than two months before the nation as a whole made its declaration. This was not entirely another instance of Vermont going its own way, however. At the time, 50,000 servicemen were on active duty, called up for the draft the year before. Because President Roosevelt had ordered the U.S. Navy to shoot first if German warships entered U.S. waters, Vermont lawmakers interpreted this as a declaration of war, which enabled them to vote a $10 monthly bonus to the draftees and help their families through a difficult situation. (Ten bucks went a lot further then than it does today—we're talking just over $176!)

In 2006, a group of dissatisfied citizens was formed, "dedicated to the proposition that Vermonters should peaceably secede from the United States and govern themselves as an independent republic once again." Now what is this group of Vermonters riled up about these days? For more information see www.commonsnews.org. ♣

THE TRAIL THAT INSPIRED THE APPALACHIAN TRAIL

The Long Trail shares a route with the younger Appalachian Trail until the two walkways part company just north of Sherburne Center, about 100 miles north of the Massachusetts border.

If you want to get a feel for Vermont's geography, geology, topography, flora, and fauna, here's a walk you might consider. The downside is that you'll need to set aside four to six weeks to complete it, if you want to earn "end-to-ender" status. This is the Long Trail, which follows the spine of the Green Mountains for 272 miles, from Massachusetts to Quebec.

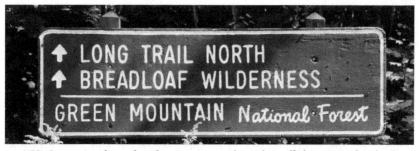

A Vermont Academy headmaster gets a big idea off the ground, which just happens to be the oldest long-distance trail in the United States.

But let's say you don't have six weeks or need more information before you make a commitment. The Green Mountain Club, which protects and maintains the trail, has created a way to test-drive the Long Trail and learn more about the experience. Visit its head-quarters (website and other contact information at the end of this story), talk to staff members, look over the trail guides and maps, and conquer the Short Trail, a half-mile loop and microcosm of the total experience. Now you're ready for any number of day hikes, as well.

This "footpath in the wilderness" occurred to Vermont out-doorsman James P. Taylor more than a hundred years ago as he waited for the fog to lift during a hike on Stratton Mountain. To get things moving Taylor, assistant headmaster of Vermont Academy, in Saxtons River, founded the Green Mountain Club (GMC) in 1910 and was its first president. Over the next twenty years, a 272-mile path was cleared, hitting just about every summit along the way, from Consultation Peak near the Massachusetts border to Mount Carleton, just south of the Canadian border. Today seventy huts and shelters 8 to 10 miles apart provide overnight cover, protection from the weather, and a dry place to prepare meals. The Long Trail map identifies 185 miles of 1- to 5-mile access trails, a few of which can also serve as loop trails for day hikes. The GMC also has identified six supply stations—grocery, post office, and bar-and-grill stops at 45- to 55-mile intervals—to provide basic services and sustenance. Some 200,000 hikers trek the Long Trail yearly, and more than one hundred of them make it from end to end.

The Long Trail shares its southernmost 100 miles with the better-known Appalachian Trail. The two trails part company just north of U.S. Route 4 near Sherburne Center. The Long Trail then continues north to Canada, and the AT veers east to New Hampshire and Maine. The Long Trail is credited with being the inspiration for the younger, longer AT. Now here's a conundrum: In 1900, ten years before James Taylor's Stratton Mountain epiphany, AT founder Benton MacKaye claimed to have been identically inspired by a Stratton Mountain vision. Twenty-one years then went by before MacKaye published his AT proposal, at just about the same time the Long Trail was completed. Why? To be kind (and not gratuitously nosy), no one seems to know. Visions are tricky, one must assume—and illusory, for sure.

During its history the GMC has been vigorously proactive in preserving the wilderness character of the Long Trail. When a scenic highway the length of the Green Mountain Range was proposed in the mid-1930s, the club mounted a spirited enough opposition to cause its rejection in a statewide referendum. A planned missile communications facility on Mount Mansfield in 1958 met the same fate in the face of club resistance. The GMC has conserved more than 25,000 acres of Long Trail lands, many of which have been added to Vermont's state forests. More than 800 volunteers aid GMC staffers in keeping an eye on trails and making repairs when needed.

One of the most demanding sections of the trail is the ascent of Mount Mansfield, north of Stowe and crossing Route 108 in an area known as Smugglers' Notch. Actually, Mount Mansfield claims six peaks, which together are said to resemble the head and neck of a giant in repose. (The Abenaki thought it rather the profile of a moose head. Make up your own mind when you get there.)

Writer Bill Scheller and friend Rich Mara hike the Long Trail every year, usually in November because they have the trail and shelters all to themselves. Following is an excerpt from Bill's account of his 2007 ascent to Mt. Mansfield's "chin," at 4,393 feet the highest point in Vermont. The complete story, "Up and Across Mt. Mansfield," appears in www. naturaltraveler.com (click on "Archives" to find the 11/16/07 issue).

"The Long Trail itself, once it ascends beyond tree line at this end of Mansfield, boldly pushes itself and its plucky trekkers to the threshold of technical climbing. At several points, with the Chin summit tantalizingly within view, we were forced to ascend on hands and knees, always remembering that backpacks play havoc with one's center of gravity. One spot was particularly challenging: You had to plant your knees on a rock shelf as wide as your knees. This made for a fine puzzle, as the next thing you had to do was get a foot up onto the space already occupied by your knees, or at least one of them. I don't recall how I did it, but I remember that the alternative would have been to stay there forever like a stunted pine, or hope that a ledge, ten feet below would have impeded my descent to level ground, some two hundred feet down.

"The views from the Chin were worth the little frisson of doom. From the roof of Vermont, we looked east toward Mt. Washington in New Hampshire, north past Jay Peak into Quebec's Eastern Townships, and west across lowland farms and villages to Lake Champlain and the Adirondacks beyond."

Directions: The club is about 4 miles south of Stowe on the west side of Route 100. Take the next right entrance at the sign for the 1836 Cabins and Evergreen Gardens just before the GMC office. Hours vary by season. No admission charged. For more information visit www.greenmountainclub.org or call (802) 244-7037.

(Links to relevant YouTube footage appear below, as well as following selected entries in every chapter. To access any of those below that interest you, type the titles in the YouTube.com search box of your computer or mobile device.)

YOUTUBE VIDEO:
"Long Trail Thru Hike 2017" (3:50)
(Dozens more to choose from) ❀

80TH REUNION FOR A VERMONT ACADEMY LEGEND

Madeline Bergstrom

Bob Campbell demonstrates a Mitchell 16mm. camera for a Perkins School pupil with partial eyesight (circa 1975).

Five years or so after the Long Trail was finished, Maine-born and Pennsylvania-bred Bob Campbell entered Vermont Academy as a freshman, graduating in 1937. For many of the years between then and 2017, when he celebrated his 80th VA reunion, the Academy has been a central part of his life.

A few years after college, Bob and his wife Beth moved to Saxtons River, where they raised eleven children—six of whom also attended Vermont Academy. Bob was the school's first director of development, where his knack for fund-raising financed, first, the school's gymnasium, and then its dining hall—which he also helped design.

Bob's principal occupation, though, was filmmaker. As president of Campbell Films, he contracted and produced more than 100 educational motion pictures for high schools and colleges—including a half dozen or so for Perkins School for the Blind (for which he also served as consultant for 25 years). Decades later—just as he was ready to retire, in fact—the digital age took over.

One might say these two transitions worked out quite nicely. At age 99, Bob certainly would seem ready to relax a bit. Instead, he now spends much of his time working on collages and assemblages. Well played, sir!

BEASTS FROM THE DEEP

Vermont is way ahead of a lot of states in at least one respect. It is home to not one, but two lake monsters. They probably don't know each other, living as they do from 85 to 165 miles apart—depending on what part of the respective lake each happens to be swimming in.

But who's to say? Monsters differ from the rest of us in significant ways. The very label "monster," for example, indicates an otherworldly dimension and at the same time betrays our deep-seated ambivalence about whether such creatures even exist.

Take Memphré, for example, who resides—or is said to reside—in Lake Memphremagog, which straddles the United States-Canada border between Vermont and Quebec. The International Dracontology Society, originated by SCUBA diver Jacques Boisvert in 1986, has recorded 229 sightings of Memphré since then. One young woman responded this way to a story by Boisvert in the *Newport Express:*

"After reading your article I just had to write relating our own phenomenal experience. From out of nowhere appeared a brown object with a long wake. Should we believe there is a mystery serpent in Lake Memphremagog?" The animal was shiny, the woman said. She estimated it to be about 30 feet long.

Some years later: February 22, 2006, on Lake Champlain in Burlington, another story was unfolding. ABC News showed exclusive video of a reptile called Champ that fishermen had spotted just below the surface.

"It made my hair stand on end," said fisherman Dick Affolter.

"I'm 100 percent sure [that we saw something]," said fisherman Peter Bodette. "I'm just not 100 percent sure what it was."

Over the years, there have been hundreds of sightings of Champ—sometimes more than a dozen a year—going back to the early 1800s. From the various descriptions it has been speculated that the lake monster may be a reptile known as a plesiosaur, which lived in the Triassic period about 250 million years ago. If so, this would not be the first time a sea dweller thought to be extinct "came back to life." In 1938, a coelacanth (SEEL-uh-kanth), thought to be extinct along with the dinosaur some 65 million years ago, reappeared off the waters of South Africa. With a barracuda-like mouth and outward-thrusting, leg-like fins that move alternately (like a trotting horse), the bottom-feeding coelacanth is about six feet long and has a life-span of 60 years or more.

It's hard to believe that, no matter how many generations comprise 65 million years, only one each of these obviously mild-mannered monsters reaches maturity in its respective lake every 30 years or so—where might Mrs. Champ or Memphré and the kids be, for example; know what I mean? Still, because there are so many more questions than answers, this particular mystery remains alive.

(Links to relevant YouTube footage appear below, as well as following selected entries in every chapter. To access any of those below that interest you, type the titles in the YouTube.com search box of your computer or mobile device.)

YouTube Videos:
"Champ the Sea Monster of Lake Champlain" (7:45)
"America's Loch Ness Monster" (5:39)
"Thirty-foot Lake Monster of Lake Memphré" 6:20 ❦

ESCAPING VERMONT WINTERS WITHOUT MOVING A MUSCLE

Volume IV of the Bulletin of the New York Public Library lists ten separate disputes between New York and Vermont from 1780 until 1899 to fix the precise location of Vermont's western boundary. For example, in 1814 that line was moved westward some 50 feet from the border established two years earlier. According to Warren S. Patrick, one Rupert farmer affected by this particular surveyor's decision realized that his house and land were now entirely in the state of New York. "Thank God," he said to his wife. "I don't think I could stand another Vermont winter."

FREAKS OF NATURE PART I—THE FLOOD THAT CHANGED A STATE

Twenty-eight lives were lost in Bolton, near Camel's Hump, in the 1927 flood. Here a man rows away from a Bolton house on the south bank of the Winooski River.

Vermonters were looking for relief after evenly spaced storms in October, 1927 thoroughly saturated the state. Instead, on November 2, a storm from the mid-Atlantic coast met yet another from the upper Great Lakes region A high-pressure area over the state of Maine effectively held these two storms motionless over Vermont. The result was a drenching that lasted 45 consecutive hours. During that time nearly 10 inches of rain fell.

Virtually every river and stream violently overflowed its banks. Nearly 1,300 bridges were washed away. Railways and highways disappeared. Eighty-four people lost their lives. More than 9,000 were left homeless, 15,000 cattle drowned, and the total cost in property losses was $700 million in today's dollars. Eight thousand Vermonters were given food, clothing, shelter, and medical assistance.

The northern half of the state was particularly hard hit. Author R. E. Atwood, in a book published just six weeks later, was inspired to anthropomorphic heights: "As if drunk with its new-found power," Atwood wrote, "the Winooski River staggered and roared its crooked way down the valley, ripping out trees, tearing away houses, barns, bridges, and gathering livestock and even human beings into its awful arms until, spent with its Herculean effort, it passed mutteringly out into Lake Champlain."

Earlier that year President Calvin Coolidge had taken considerable heat for his lack of effort in response to an even more horrendous flood. When the Mississippi River burst through dozens of levees in every border state south of Illinois, 700,000 were estimated to have lost their homes, and the death toll reached 246. Even so, President Coolidge refused to visit the area, and declined to broadcast an appeal for relief funds on national radio.

Stung by the criticism, Coolidge appointed Commerce Secretary Herbert Hoover to be in charge of Vermont flood relief efforts when the flood struck seven months later. Hoover met with Vermont leaders on November 16 to plan for relief and reconstruction. Eight thousand Vermonters were given food, clothing, shelter, and medical assistance. A Vermont flood credit corporation was formed, awarding low-interest loans to businesses, merchants, and farmers who needed them. From federal assistance came money to rebuild bridges, dams, and roads.

With the knowledge that protecting forests in the state would help prevent floods in the future, Vermont proposed 300,000 acres for a national forest. In 1932 the 102,000-acre Green Mountain Forest was proclaimed. Seven years later an additional 160,000 acres were set aside. In 2007 Vermont's National Forest numbered 385,000 acres. In this way, the 1927 flood was responsible for reshaping the state's material, political, and social environment. For more information on the Vermont Flood of 1927, see: www.

vpr.net/episode/42038; www.northlandjournal.com/stories19.html;
www.vuhs.org/project/water.htm

YouTube Video:
"Vermont's Super-Flood" -1927" (2:21)
(Silent film; several others like it.) ❧

The Year without a Summer

The eruption in April, 1815 of Mount Tambora, on the remote island of Sumbawa in Indonesia, was the most powerful volcanic eruption in human history. Not only did 100,000 people die, but the resulting 400 million-ton gas cloud caused the earth to cool the world over—to the extent of massive crop failure and starvation the following year.

Of the month of June, 1816, David Ludlum wrote in *The Vermont Weather Book:* "On the night of the 6th, water froze an inch thick—and on the night of the 7th and morning of the 8th, a kind of sleet or exceedingly cold snow fell, attended with high wind, which measured in places where it was drifted, 18 to 20 inches in depth. Saturday morning the weather was more severe than it generally is during the storms of winter."

In July, it rained in parts of New England, but not in Vermont. A frost August 21 killed most beans, potatoes and corn, and mountains were covered with snow. September saw extensive forest fires, and a killing frost September 10 wiped out everything else. That winter, cattle starved for lack of hay. Many families moved west, thinking the weather had turned permanently. Unable to sell their land, many just left. The year became known as "Eighteen Hundred and Froze to Death."

Altogether, how much stuff came out? The eruption of Tambora produced 1.75 cubic kilometers of volcanic debris, mostly ash. How much is that? Well you could bury all of the playing surface of Fenway Park in Boston 81,544 miles deep in ash. That's 131,322 km, or two times around the world. Ai-yi-yi!

FREAKS OF NATURE, PART II

The mighty Ottaauquechee River, which over centuries carved the Quechee Gorge, also devastated part of residential Quechee during 2012's tropical storm Irene.

Eighty-four years after the Flood of 1927, Vermonters took another calamitous hit—this time from a tropical storm named Irene. They weren't alone. Residents in twelve other eastern states suffered as well; also those in more than a dozen Caribbean islands and parts of southern Canada. All told, 65 million people were affected and fifty-six lives were lost—forty-nine of them in the U.S. Total damage came to $15.6 billion.

In Vermont, Irene flooded almost every river and stream. Thirteen communities became "island villages," surrounded by water and impassable, with flooding knocking out all bridges and roadways to and from. The storm dumped eleven inches of rain on parts of the state.

Entire books will be written about devastation that rocked the state in August, 2011, affecting 225 of its 255 communities. For a closer look, let's focus on a single hard-hit town in southeastern Vermont.

Irene took out Vermont's Route 4 in many places over its 66 miles between New York and New Hampshire.

A few days before Irene pounded Vermont, Chris and Eileen Kruger, co-owners of a Rockingham, Vermont hydroelectric plant on the Williams River in Brockway Mills Gorge, were vacationing on the Caribbean island of Montserrat. Most years not enough water flows on the Williams to generate electricity in August, so it was a good time to get away.

When Hurricane Irene (as it was classified in the Caribbean) hit Montserrat a glancing blow on August 22, the Krugers took it in stride. Tropical storms in the Atlantic basin are an integral part of late-summer island living. "We put up the shutters but didn't batten down because the wind wasn't that bad," recalled Kruger. "Still, we thought it was a good idea to keep track on Weather Underground."

Over the next few days Irene moved rapidly north, making U.S. landfall on the Outer Banks of North Carolina at 120 mph. After pummeling nine coastal states, it took a hard left just north of Boston, west toward southern Vermont. Every day Chris talked with a friend who regularly relieved him when he was away. Built 30 feet into the gorge's rock and the same distance below the

Brockway Mills Road bridge, the power plant seemed impervious to nearly any calamity.

On Sunday, August 28, though, the odds for such an outcome decreased sharply. Two days of continuous rain—a record 15 inches—had raised the river level in the gorge by 20 feet, and it was still rising. Kruger's friend was monitoring the situation, and his voice on successive calls became more and more strained. Not suspecting the force of the storm, he had brought along his three young sons, and was regretting the decision.

"It's getting bad," he said to Chris about mid-afternoon.

"Shut down the generator," said Chris.

"I'll do it now." After a minute he came back on the phone. "Water's coming in the window above the turbine generator."

"Are the sandbags up?"

"It's too late. Too much water coming in!"

And a minute later: "It's getting higher. Rocks are hitting the powerhouse roof!"

"Pull the breaker on the wall and get the hell out of there!" yelled Chris.

Father and sons all made it up the catwalk adjacent to the bridge without much time to spare before the rising water cut off escape options. Minutes later, local police arrived to tape off the area and keep onlookers away from the bridge. "When he told me rocks were hitting the roof," Chris said months later, "I realized the water was moving so fast it was propelling rocks and gravel along with it, from both the bottom and the banks on either side."

In just two days, 15 inches of rain—more than in the 1927 flood—had increased the flow-rate at Brockway Mills dam from 56 cubic feet per second (cfs) to 48,600. It takes 180 cfs or more to generate the two million kilowatt hours of power supplied annually to Rockingham.)

When the Krugers got home they found a submerged powerhouse filled with five feet of mud, and two feet of debris covering the outside wall and upper turbine room. Flying rocks had permanently warped the catwalk; two 1,000-pound welding machines used as backup power were washed away; as were thousands of dollars of spare parts gathered since the couple moved there in 1999. It took a year for them to get back up and running. (P.S. Chris had no insurance.)

But it wasn't just the powerhouse that felt Irene's wrath. Downstream a mile from Brockway Mills Gorge at about the same time water was approaching bridge level, resident Bill Robinson watched the house he had built, including a safe holding both gold and cash saved for his retirement, engulfed by the rapidly rising river. He took little solace when a neighbor complimented him on the quality of his workmanship as the intact house floated away.

About a mile upstream from the bridge, the 141-year-old South Bartonsville covered bridge suffered the same fate. In that instance, all was not lost. Months later, and just after the bridge was rebuilt, Chris was able to retrieve two dozen or so of the 2" x 12" spruce and hemlock planks torn from the bridge, which had come to rest on the shore across from his plant—nearly 40 feet above the river's natural level.

Five miles to the south on the Saxtons River (running parallel to the Williams), Irene did even more damage to Saxtons River village, a bit more heavily populated part of Rockingham. In addition to a damaged covered bridge and several houses carried away, firewood supplier Tom Lockerby's home and business on the bank of the river both took a critical hit. Sixteen cords of birch and oak have long since made their way to the Connecticut River and likely on to Long Island Sound in New York.

More: "Lessons from Irene: Build Resiliency as We Rebuild" (Vermont Agency of Natural Resources)

YouTube Videos:
"Brockway Mills Gorge on a Regular Day" (:53)
"Brockway Mills Gorge during Hurricane Irene" (2:56)
"Caught on tape: Irene's Flooding Takes out Bridge" (:41)
"Irene's Flooding Overtakes Vermont Town" (2:56) ❧

VERMONT WEATHER EXTREMES

The coldest weather ever recorded in Vermont was 50 degrees below zero Fahrenheit in Bloomfield, Essex County, on December 30, 1933. The warmest was 105 degrees in Vernon in the southeast corner of the state on July 4, 1911. The greatest amount of snow from a single storm—50 inches in three days—fell on Readsboro in Bennington Country on March 2-5, 1947. The greatest snowfall total for a single season was 318.6 inches (26 ½ feet) in 1970-71.

CLIMATE CHANGE—THE GLOBAL UPHEAVAL THAT AFFECTS US ALL

Bill McKibben (center right, hand on banner) and fellow activists in Washington, D.C. at the first national climate change rally in 2013.

Vermont, like 49 other states and most of the world's countries, both fights climate change and prepares for its consequences—whatever they may be. In 1989, Bill McKibben, author and Middlebury College

Schumann Distinguished Scholar, wrote The End of Nature, *called by many the first book on global warming for a general audience. In 2006, along with seven Middlebury students, he put his words into action. Here's Bill's story, written for* Vermont . . . Who Knew? *of the launching of 350.org, the group they founded to help halt this nature-ending threat—a movement now active on all seven continents.*

What has become the biggest grassroots global climate movement began in 2006 at the Robert Frost rest area on Rte. 125 in Ripton, Vermont. There we gathered to begin a five-day march to Burlington for action on climate change. It was good fun in itself—lots of conversations, lots of good potluck suppers, and by the time we got to Burlington, where Bernie greeted us, we were a thousand marchers. But it was a news item the next day that really got us going. Those thousand marchers, the *Free Press* reported, constituted the largest demonstration about climate change that had yet taken place in America.

No wonder we were losing, we thought. We had all the component parts of a movement: the scientists, the policy people, Al Gore. We had just forgotten the movement part. And so we set about to change that. "We" in this case being seven undergraduates at Middlebury College and myself. We made our first effort at broadening the fight in Vermont: a fall day when we coordinated demonstrations in iconic locations across the state (I gave a talk by cellphone from the summit of Camel's Hump). And then we took on the nation. In the fall of 2007, we coordinated 1,500 demonstrations in all fifty states, a show of force that we called Step it Up, and which persuaded then-Democratic candidates Hillary Clinton and Barack Obama to increase their focus on global warming.

And then we went after the world, launching 350.org from the college dining hall in early 2008. Our name came from the newest climate science, which showed that 350 parts per million of carbon dioxide was the most we could safely have in the atmosphere (a number we're already well north of, hence the melting Arctic, rising ocean, and so on). We chose it in part because we wanted to organize the whole world and figured Arabic numerals would be easier than English words. Each of the seven students took a continent (the guy who got Antarctica also got the internet) and off we went. It was, of course, absurd. And yet beginners luck is a real thing. It worked pretty well right from the start: That next fall we coordinated a day of action with 5,200 rallies in 181 countries, what CNN called "the most widespread day of political action in the planet's history." From the top of Antarctica's highest mountain to the most remote part of Africa's Masai country, from the center of Manhattan to the steppes of Mongolia; everyone shared the same message. Over time we've gone on to start the fight against new fossil fuel infrastructure with the Keystone pipeline battle, helped organize the largest climate march on the planet (400,000 people on the streets of New York), and began the massive fossil fuel divestment push that has now persuaded portfolios worth $6 trillion from oil and gas and coal stocks. This hasn't stopped climate change—the planet is still warming—but it is turning a rout into a fight.

And it all began on the western edge of Vermont, with a march up Route 7 and a bunch of long meetings in a college dining hall. In the subsequent years, we've always counted on Vermonters to punch way above their weight. I'll never forget being in D.C. for the start of those giant Keystone protests, with hundreds of people headed off to jail every day. A bus pulled up one morning, and out stepped fifty Vermonters—it had taken them all day and all night to get there, because two days earlier Hurricane Irene had ripped apart the state, closing most of the roads and bridges. "We knew it was too late to stop that storm, said one of the Vermonters as she stepped off the bus. "We wanted to stop the next one."

———————

The present as prologue: Many climate-change deniers believe as they do because such change occurs so slowly it is imperceptible day to day—often even year to year. Nevertheless, individual incidents can demonstrate what may be in store for us, until or unless we change our ways. Each of the three years before this book's publication has been hotter on average than the one preceding it. (Take note of this phenomenon for future reference. Bill McKibben tells us in his account above that 350.

org was named for the number of parts per million of carbon dioxide that is safe for us to have in the atmosphere. On August 17, 2018, that figure was 407.09. This means that to turn the situation around—or even to slow it down—we all have to work harder: as individuals, as families, as communities, and both nationally and in cooperation with other nations. Find out how you can do your part—and then teach others to do theirs.

YOUTUBE VIDEO:
Bill McKibben's Climate Change March (2:38)
(Trailer for 55-minute film of four-day march to Burlington (www.jancannonfilms.com)

350.org – "Climate Change Is About Power" (2:18) ♣

BUG ADVENTURES FOR A WORTHY CAUSE

From age 11 growing up in Sparks, Maryland, Jordan Fletcher was experimental—as well as a bit of a daredevil. He was a tree climber, as are most kids, but he and a friend improvised a "bosun's chair" (sort of a climbing harness) they could throw over branches above them and then pull themselves up to heights they wouldn't otherwise have reached.

As an adult, Jordan continued to experiment, learning soon enough that his philosophy major at the University of Maryland had only begun to prepare him for a gratifying career. The question was: Did that career even exist? Jordan remembered the words of Joseph Campbell and "followed his bliss." Over the next decade his occupations included —in no particular order—emergency medical technician, elementary school science teacher, canoe guide, river guide, tower climber, high ropes guide, and furniture maker.

One day after making furniture, Jordan's wife Sheryl surprised him. It was 2005 and they were living in Montpelier. Sheryl, a fabric artist and freelance editor, knew well he was sick of his job—and also his interest in climbing.

courtesy of the author

Jordan plots his next move during the removal of a diseased ash tree.

Mitch Moraksi

2014 Volunteer Group - Vermont Tree Steward
Recognized by the Vermont Urban and Community Forestry Council

The Fletcher Family
Jordan, Sheryl, Liam and Aiden

"The Fletcher family aka "Fletcher Clan" is so very deserving of a Vermont Steward award for their dedicated, meaningful and perpetual volunteer work and their eternal readiness to lend a helping hand."

Trish Hanson, Nominator

Sheryl, behind sons Liam (left) and Aiden, in 2008 at the Montpelier North Branch Nature Center "BioBlitz."

"This sounds interesting," she said, showing Jordan a help-wanted ad for an arborist intern. He agreed, interviewed, and got the job. For some months, though, his responsibilities were limited to cleaning up after tree removals: raking up debris and feeding the wood chipper.

The first day he went up a tree, his colleagues were amazed at his mountain-goat-level skills. When he heard "We didn't know you could climb like that!" he said, "Well, I told you enough times," and let it go at that. Just after his first full year on the job, Jordan realized he could do better on his own, and in 2006 he started Fletcher Tree Service.

The Fletchers, now including sons Liam and Aiden, moved south to Westminster West, near Putney, and business grew quickly. Jordan committed himself to old-school practices. He works alone and without any modern aids, except of course chain saws and his truck. Planning a removal includes a close examination of the tree—and the extent to which it will support his weight climbing to make the cuts. "You learn as much about a tree's health from its base as you would from the skin of a person," says Jordan.

Vermont arborists, like those in other northern states, are virtually work-free from December through March. That time, of course, can be spent in many ways. Jordan chose volunteering, and quickly settled on a cause. The emerald ash borer (EAB) is a beetle that has destroyed millions of ash trees, and has made its way from Asia to the United States, first in Michigan in 2002 and now also the Northeast, including Vermont.

All of this was well known to Jordan, who when the family still lived in Montpelier, had joined the Vermont Entomological Society. Through this group the Fletchers met affable and committed professionals, some of whom also worked in the state's Department of Forests, Parks, and Recreation. Both Liam and Aiden learned excellent netting skills. Entomologist Trish Hanson shared her enthusiasm, and traded books with Sheryl about their respective interests. Jordan worked with Jim Esden, a forester in Vermont's forest health program, helping to slow the spread of a hemlock nemesis, and later the EAB. Two years or so later all four Fletchers could legitimately be labeled citizen-scientists.

One of their tasks was to locate and gather data on the EAB's principal predator. The smoky winged beetle bandit wasp (*Cerceris fumipennis)* hunts several kinds of wood-boring beetles, including the EAB, and carries them back to its nest to feed its young. If an ash borer is near, the *Cerceris* wasp will likely capture it. If so, the stunned beetle often will be found nearby. Many wasps are netted in flight on the way back to their nest, beetle in tow.

In 2014, the Vermont Dept. of Forests, Parks &Recreation honored the Fletchers as Tree Steward Volunteer Group of the Year. It was a complete shock then, when Sheryl was diagnosed with brain cancer earlier that year. "Sher is too weak to travel," Jordan wrote Trish in apology for not being able to attend the award ceremony in December, "and the boys don't want to go without their Mom since she was instrumental in the survey"

Part of Trish Hanson's award copy appearing in the program's newsletter the following month went as follows: "The Vermont Urban and Community Forestry Program was pleased to present the Fletcher family with the Volunteer Group Tree Steward Award at the Vermont Statehouse December 17, 2014. The family has been exceedingly generous with its time and energy in a variety of volunteer projects, particularly the *Cerceris* wasp biosurveillance program. Thus far, they have completed their work in three communities. We are saddened to say that on January 3, 2015, Sheryl lost in her brave struggle against cancer, surrounded by her family." (Two months earlier, Trish, on behalf of the Department of Forests, Parks & Recreation, designated the Fletcher family to be "cause of the year," and conducted a fund-raising effort to defray expenses resulting from Sheryl's illness.)

With understandable difficulty, Jordan, Liam, and Aiden have been able to move on. Jordan continues to work with trees. All three have great memories of the years when the Fletcher clan did its part assisting the Vermont Department of Forests, Parks, and Recreation. Jordan much appreciates the guidance and camaraderie of the splendid team he worked with—including forest pest program coordinators Barbara Schultz and Caitlin Cusack.

YOUTUBE VIDEO:
"Netting Wasps to Fight Emerald Ash Borer" (2:32)
(WCCO CBS Minnesota) ❦

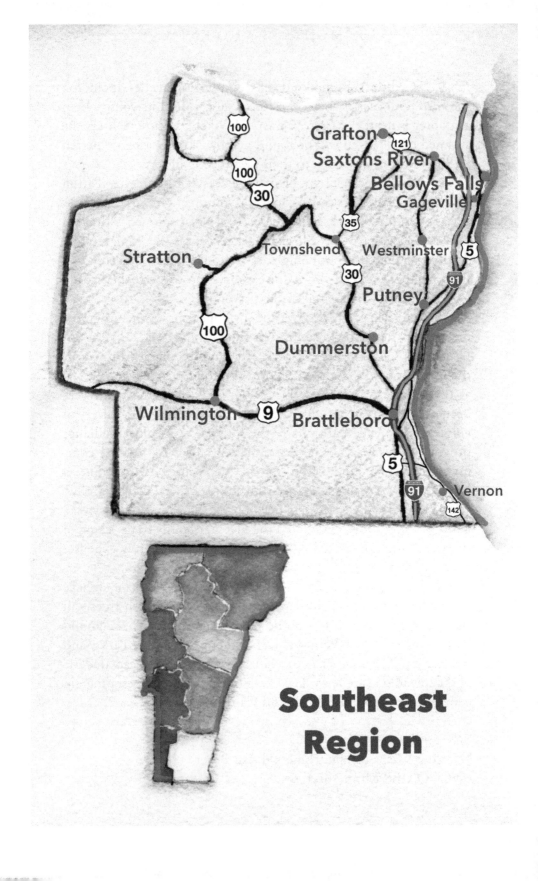

Grafton

Saxtons River

Bellows Falls

Gageville

100

100

30

35

Townshend

Westminster

5

Stratton

30

91

100

Putney

Dummerston

Wilmington

9

Brattleboro

5

91

Vernon

142

**Southeast
Region**

2

SOUTHEAST

It's part of the "Banana Belt" to Vermonters living to the north, largely because the snow usually disappears as early as May 1, and consecutive days below zero less frequently reach double digits. But there are non-meteorological attributes to be highlighted as well. Paul Simon's percussionist had his drums made here. One of the towns was named for its surveyor, who—in establishing original boundaries—walked backward into the river that bears his name and drowned.

What else . . . Rudyard Kipling wrote some of his best work in Dummerston, before he was driven out of the country. Oh yes, you'll find out why. And one of our nation's richest women ever (richer even than Oprah Winfrey) became known more for her ability to pinch pennies than as the Wall Street tycoon she became. She was so cheap, in fact, that she relied solely on free health clinics to treat her son for a leg infection that ultimately resulted in an amputation. (He got even, though!) And speaking of being careful with pennies, only a U.S. senator from Vermont could have conducted his entire election campaign for a total cost of $1.08. That would be George Aiken.

By the way, you probably didn't know you could get some of the best barbecue in the country here, did you? This isn't idle hype; Gourmet magazine said so. It's all here, folks.

A BRIDGE NOT FAR ENOUGH

Bellows Falls

The Vilas Bridge, looking west to Vermont from New Hampshire.

About 30 feet along the south side of Bellows Falls' Vilas Bridge, just above the waterline, are two fading yellow paint stripes about 10 feet apart, each indicating the location of eight to twelve faces carved into the rock. Depending on which researcher you talk to they are thought to be prehistoric Indian carvings 2,000 or more years old, or only 300 years old but possibly commemorating a battle with settlers in the early 1700s. The dating was made difficult by the good intentions of the local chapter of the Daughters of the Revolution who decided to deepen the carvings to make them more visible. No comment.

An unpleasant situation regarding the Vilas Bridge makes viewing the petroglyphs a bit difficult—if not downright impossible. First of all, the bridge is closed—and has been since 2009. Not quite what you'd expect as a "symbol of friendship" between New Hampshire and Vermont since 1930. For the next 79 years, 4,000-5,000 vehicles crossed the Vilas Bridge daily. In 2009, though, a lack of maintenance by the New Hampshire Department of Transportation caused so much deterioration that the reinforced concrete bridge had to be shut down.

The *way* back story: In 1764, King George III whimsically handed over Vermont to New Hampshire and New York to carve up on their own. (This is one reason Vermont seceded from the colonies in the first place—see Chapter 1.) New Hampshire wound up with the Connecticut River, all the way to the low-water mark on the west bank. For this prize, New Hampshire agreed to complete and pay for all repairs to bistate bridges over the Connecticut River. Its record for handling the repair side of the deal, though, has been, let's say, "spotty."

Since 2009, the two states' representatives have met in several attempts to reach an agreement. In 2014, the state of Vermont offered to pay an estimated $5-$6 million to rehabilitate the Vilas, in exchange for New Hampshire meantime paying to repair other bridges between the two states until the Vilas job was completed. New Hampshire declined the Vermont offer, and as of late-2018, had not made one of its own.

Directions: If you are driving north on U.S. Route 5, turn right on Westminster Street, and right again 2 blocks farther on Bridge Street. Park in one of the spaces in front of the Bellows Falls Post Office. Or drive east another 100 yards, turning right into the abandoned railroad spur opposite the Indian carvings sign. Note: The carvings are often underwater during spring runoff in March and April.

YOUTUBE VIDEO:
"Vermonters Take Vilas Bridge!" (4:14)
(The Green Mtn Boyz 2.0 in Action) ✤

HETTY GREEN, RICHEST WOMAN IN THE WORLD

Bellows Falls

Hetty Green's tough negotiating tactics earned her the nickname "Witch of Wall Street." They also made her the richest woman in the world

Adjusted for twenty-first-century dollars, Hetty Green is the richest American woman in history. Her fortune when she died in 1916 was estimated at $200 million, which in today's dollars is $4.8 billion—more than Oprah Winfrey, by some. Yet she is remembered today for her eccentricities rather than for her billions.

Hetty Howland Robinson was born in New Bedford, Massachusetts, in 1834. Her father and grandfather were millionaire owners of a large whaling fleet. At age six she could read the day's financial papers; at eight she opened her first savings account. When her father died, he left Hetty $7.5 million, much of which she invested in railroads and real estate.

In her early thirties Hetty met and married Edward Green, a wealthy silk and tea trader who had spent twenty years in the Orient. They had two children, Ned and Sylvia, and moved to Edward's family home in Bellows Falls. Hetty did not change the penny-pinching ways she developed as a child: She walked blocks to buy broken cookies in bulk, returned her berry boxes for a nickel, carried a small can to get the best price on milk for her cat, and once spent hours looking for a two-cent stamp. Though most of her eccentric behavior was viewed as harmless, she once refused to pay a doctor to treat Ned's knee, dislocated in a sledding accident with the damage exacerbated a year later when he was hit by a wagon pulled by a Saint Bernard. When treatment at free clinics failed, Ned's leg was amputated.

Hetty and Edward divorced after Edward's business investments went sour, with Hetty immediately invoking a very favorable pre-nup. When she died at age eight-one, her entire estate went to her two children, both of whom took a strikingly different view of handling money. Sylvia gave the rundown Green family home to the town of Bellows Falls. The site, at the corner of Westminster and Church Streets, is now occupied by a bank, a municipal parking lot, and Hetty Green Park. She also donated $1 million for a new Bellows Falls hospital.

Brother Ned, one might say, went his own direction. After getting his law degree at Fordham, he managed Hetty's real estate affairs in Chicago, and then was sent to Texas to revivify a railroad she had bought for next to nothing. Along with Colonel Green (as he was then called) went Mabel Harlow, a prostitute who became his companion—and after a disapproving Hetty died, his wife. Ned, by then a striking 6'4" and 300 pounds—and on a single leg—amassed millions, thanks both to Hetty's head start and his own business acumen. Without his mother to dictate otherwise, moreover, he was pretty well able to spend the better part of it just as he wanted,

Directly across School Street from Hetty Green Park (behind the bank) is Immanuel Episcopal Church and its adjacent cemetery at the end of Church Street, where Hetty, her husband, children, and in-laws are buried. Their 8-foot-high obelisk monument is in the lower cemetery just off the sidewalk, between two tall trees and halfway from either entrance. ✤

FIRST CANAL IN THE UNITED STATES

New York's Erie Canal, which opened in 1825, is perhaps the best-known U.S. canal, but the canal system that realized the dream of mass transportation of goods throughout the country began in Vermont more than two decades earlier. The Erie Canal was called the engineering marvel of the nineteenth century. But if you go into Bellows Falls, you'll see a plaque that appears near a bridge over the first canal, designed and built by Samuel Morey, of Fairlee. (That's not all this accomplished man was famous for, as you'll see on page 143.)

BELLOWS FALLS CANAL

Here first canal in United States was built in 1802.

The British-owned company which was chartered to render the Connecticut River navigable here in 1791

Was ten years building the nine locks and dam

Around the Great Falls, 52-feet high.

After the first railroad came through Bellows Falls in 1849, river traffic declined sharply, and the canal has been used ever since for water power only. More than 200 years later, the canal is chugging away, although it is somewhat deeper and wider.

Directions: The Bellows Falls Canal plaque is near the bridge on Bridge Street, 100 yards or so west of the directional sign for the Indian Carvings. ✤

TRANSCENDING THE CIGAR-BOX GUITAR REVOLUTION

Darrell, with tools of revolution assembled.

Darrell Ward, grocery produce manager at Saxtons River's Village Market by day, has been a woodworking specialist in his spare hours for the past 20 years. For a good part of this time he refinished furniture, but for the last few years Darrell has used his talents to make musical instruments. Carefully noting the extent of the "Cigar-Box Guitar Revolution," he made sure they became part of his repertoire.

But recently, Ward noticed that cigar-box guitar sales may have peaked. In a moment of pure inspiration, he came up with that particular instrument's successor: Enter the bedpan banjo. The sublime resonance is just where he wants it, and its funk-quotient is impossible to deny.

Now it's just a matter of catching on with the public. If for some reason that doesn't happen, though, Darrell's ski-tip fiddle is waiting patiently for its moment in the sun. All you angel investors out there, take heed! And those of you who think strumming your own bedpan banjo is an activity of possible interest, whether for pleasure or for profit, Darrel is available to affirm your decision at 802.463.9442.

FORT DUMMER, VERMONT'S FIRST NONTRIBAL SETTLEMENT

Brattleboro

After crossing the Vermont-Massachusetts border from the south on Interstate 91, your first landmark, up on the right, will be the entrance sign to Fort Dummer State Park. These days, Vermont residents have little need for a fort to protect their turf. Disputes between Vermont and New Hampshire folks, for example—other than the Vilas Bridge, have been largely restricted to complaints by Vermonters that a planned New Hampshire Wal-Mart expansion across the river from Brattleboro was thought to be a travesty, leading to potential traffic jams across the border.

Back in the eighteenth century, though, matters were a bit more serious. Fort Dummer was built in 1724 along the banks of the Connecticut River to protect what was then a Massachusetts colony from invasions by the French and Indians. The Salmon Hole Massacre of 1748, for example, was one of hundreds of skirmishes that took place during King George's War, from 1744–1748.

Early one May morning, eighty soldiers led by Captain Eleazer Melvin, of Northfield, Massachusetts, were three weeks into a scouting expedition from Fort Dummer. They stopped at the headwaters of the West River, in Londonderry, believing they had outrun their French and Indian pursuers. Stripping off their packs, they stopped to rest a bit and shoot a few salmon for breakfast. Two French soldiers and nine Indians who had been close behind them heard the shots and quickly located their adversaries. They opened fire from behind logs and trees, killing six soldiers. While killing but six of a group of eighty stretches the definition of *massacre* a bit, you must admit that a confrontation named the "Salmon Hole Massacre" sure has an intriguing ring to it.

Today's park overlooks the site of Fort Dummer, which was flooded when the Vernon Dam was built in 1908. The fort is now underwater, near a lumber company on the Vermont side of the river. The campground, located in the southern foothills of the Green Mountains, includes fifty-one tent/trailer sites and ten lean-to sites along with hot showers but no trailer hookups. Also in the park are a picnic area and hiking trails.

Directions: From I-91, take exit 1. Go 1/10 mile north on U.S. Route 5A, and then go 1/2 mile east on Fairground Road, and finally 1 mile south on Main Street and Old Guilford Road. For more information visit www.vtstateparks.com/htm/fortdummer.cfm.

YOUTUBE PHOTOS
"Vermont State Parks Photos: Fort Dummer State Park (:33)" ❧

GOT MILK?

The 162,000 cows living on Vermont farms are said to produce more than 2.6 billion pounds of milk a year—or more than 16,000 pounds per cow. We'll help you with the math: That's forty-four pounds per cow per day.

STROLLING OF THE HEIFERS

You've heard, perhaps, of the Running of the Bulls, in Pamplona? On eight consecutive days every July at 8:00 a.m., a rocket alerts this entire Spanish town to the awareness that two dozen cranky, 1300-pound bulls have been released on a closed, half-mile-long public street. Their goal: To vent their fury and frustration on the abysmally slower and imprudent two-legged creatures who for their own reasons are trying to outrun them.

"Strolling of the Heifers" kicks off Brattleboro National Dairy Month as a salute to family farms and their contributions to Vermont's agricultural heritage.

But what Brattleboro's annual June "Strolling of the Heifers" festival lacks in melodrama and derring-do (people have been killed during the masochistic spectacle held a month later and 3,500 miles away), it more than compensates with its pure celebration of a rural way of life, and an expression of gratitude to the farmers who drive it.

The highlight, of course, is the iconic parade: 100 flower-laden Holstein and Jersey cows—and occasionally a Guernsey or two—making their way down Main Street to a cheering crowd, followed by draft horses, tractors, jugglers, clowns, and fire-eaters. But it wouldn't be a dairy festival without a milking contest, music by the Heifer Brass Quartet (and at least a dozen other jazz and classical groups), a Dairy Princess Pageant, and a Royal Farmers Feast and Farm Tour. Many festival-goers are sure to be in town the night before the parade, when local farm families are honored for the decades of work they've done to keep southern Vermont's agricultural tradition alive.

So, the Strolling of the Heifers not only kicks off National Dairy Month each June but is a way to protect and promote Vermont's agricultural heritage in residents' daily lives. After raising more than a half-million dollars over the years for educational programs in more than 80 Windham County schools, SOTH is now focused on creating a new generation of sustainable agricultural specialists. Windham Grows, its new training and mentoring center, has a goal over the next ten years to build 85 food and agricultural businesses employing 1000 people, and attracting $45 million in private investment. Follow their progress at www.strollingoftheheifers.com/windhamgrows

YOUTUBE VIDEO
"Strolling of the Heifers - The 5-Minute Version" (4:54)
(A parade for those who prefer participants to pick up the pace.) ❦

VERMONT—MOST RURAL STATE IN THE NATION

The definition of "rural," at least in Vermont, depends on the number of people who live in places with fewer than 2,500 people. Because most of Vermont's 255 cities, towns, and gores hold fewer than 2,500 residents, the state is by definition rural. Services and elected officials usually follow these local boundaries. Unlike most states, In which counties are used to determine rural and urban populations, Vermont's fourteen counties are organized only to provide law enforcement and judicial services. No other governmental services exist at the county level.

BRATTLEBORO, HOME OF ART DECO

Brattleboro

The Latchis Hotel and Theatre is one of only two Art Deco buildings in the state of Vermont. When the movie house was built in 1938, it was the centerpiece of a fourteen-theater complex throughout New England created by Peter Latchis and his Greek immigrant father, Demetrius, who sold fruit from a pushcart as his first job in the United States.

The theatre portion of the Latchis Hotel and Theatre was designed in a Greek mythology theme. Ask about the Latchis "Dinner and a Movie" package for an evening-long treat.

In 2003 the Brattleboro Arts Initiative joined in buying the building from the Latchis family to restore the theater and hotel to create a first-rate center for the arts in downtown Brattleboro.

The main theater—there are also two smaller screening rooms, with another one yet planned—is dominated by Doric-columned facades of Greek temple replicas on both sides of the room. The ceiling is a light blue, bedecked with sparkling stars and the twelve signs of the zodiac. Continuing the art nouveau interior is a tableau of the lovable Leto and her infants, Apollo and Artemis.

Directions: To reach the Latchis Hotel and Theatre, at 50 Main Street, from I-91, use exit 2 and take Route 9 east toward town. Follow Route 9 as it becomes Western Avenue and then High Street, until it intersects Main. Take a right and go 2 blocks to the corner of Flat Street. For more information on the hotel complete descriptions of their variety of bargain packages, visit www.latchis. com, or call (800) 798-6301. ❧

A FAMILY TRADITION REKINDLED

Brattleboro

Christian Stromberg was halfway through construction of his new barn in the village of Cambridge-port, on the Saxtons River, when he realized that it offered more space than he needed. He was also at a career crossroad, not really sure if metallurgical engineering was his true lifework.

While considering, Christian recalled conversations with his grandfather many decades before. The family had fled Czarist Lithuania in 1906, and while assimilating smoothly into American society, they also had preserved a few Lithuanian traditions and customs, among them the production of fine liqueurs. The stories Christian's grandfather told about the process, as well as the satisfaction it evoked, made his decision an easy one.

Since 2006—exactly a century from the year of the family's U.S. arrival—Christian and a staff of four at Saxtons River Distillery have carried on the tradition of producing fine liqueurs by, as he says, "combining old world heritage with the flavors of Vermont."

Reviewer Christopher Null describes the company's Sapling Maple Bourbon as "A combination of Madeira, tawny Port, cinnamon, and rum raisin notes. . . . The thick syrup character that makes up the body feels like it was just tapped from the tree."

New York Times writer Florence Fabricant concurred in an equally flowery tribute, calling the product a "darker, woodsier Vermont maple bourbon whiskey," and "lovely for after-dinner sipping." But don't just listen to the media. In 2011, Sapling won a gold medal at the World Spirits Competition in San Francisco. In 2015, it received yet another top San Francisco award for its Perk Coffee Liqueur—made with locally roasted Mocha Joe's coffee.

Corporate growing pains forced Christian and his staff out of the once-too-big Cambridgeport barn in 2011 into new quarters in Brattleboro, 25 miles south. All four found homes near enough to their new digs to bike to work on nice days. Christian also walks his son and daughter to class—both in elementary school—before hopping on his own bike to start nice work days.

But wait: Recent increased production has already doomed the new physical plant as too small. Snowdrop Gin, the newest SR Distillery product, now takes up much of the scant remaining space (It also sounds like a winner, with a 93-point ranking from *Wine Enthusiast* magazine—which translates to "excellent, highly recommended.").

One has to believe that somewhere, the grandfather responsible for inspiring Christian's success is saluting his grandson with an enthusiastic thumbs-up.

Saxtons River Distillery, 485 West River Road, Brattleboro, VT. 802.246.1128. www.saplingliqueur.com Directions to the tasting room: I-91 to Exit 2; Route 9 East toward Brattleboro; Left at stop light onto Main Street; Follow signs to Route 30; two miles North on Route 30; 485 is on the right

YouTube Video:
"Saxtons River Distillery": Six videos on aspects of the distilling process, all under 1:00 ❧

Indian British Yankee Go Home!

Dummerston

In 1892, at the age of twenty-seven, poet and novelist Rudyard Kipling married an American girl and moved from London to Dummerston, Vermont, just north of Brattleboro. Kipling already was internationally famous when he married Caroline Balestier, whose recently deceased brother had been Kipling's good friend. The couple built a grand house with a distant view of New Hampshire's Mount Monadnock, near Carrie's parents' home. Kipling, who was a British subject born in India, named his new home Naulakha, Indian for "precious jewel"—and also the title of a book he wrote with his wife's brother, Wolcott.

Rudyard Kipling named his house in Vermont "Naulakha," from the title of a book he wrote with American friend Wolcott Balestier—whose sister he later married.

In just a few months, Kipling began receiving more mail in Dummerston than the largest business in nearby Brattleboro. U.S. Postmaster General Wilson authorized a special post office (to this day, it is said, the only one ever created for an individual) to handle the author's letters and packages. "Waite, Vermont" was located in the home of Kipling's neighbor, Anna Waite, who was also appointed postmaster. The Waite postmark has been prized by philatelists for more than a century.

Kipling loved his time in Vermont, and at Naulakha over the next four years, he wrote the *Jungle Book* and *Captains Courageous* and began work on *Kim* and the *Just So Stories*. He had friends in Brattleboro, and frequently played poker at the Brooks House Tower Room. To his calloused, hardworking farmer neighbors, however, Kipling was thought to be a man who "didn't work," and who spent inordinate amounts of time playing with his two little girls, Josephine and Elsie. (In his spare time he also designed what is believed to be the first tennis court in Vermont and painted golf balls red to "invent" winter golf.)

Eventually, Kipling's dream life became a nightmare. Carrie had a serious falling-out with her other brother, Beatty, who was described variously as a "feckless alcoholic" and unmatched in "sheer boorishness." A lurid lawsuit, trial, and much negative publicity followed the muscular Beatty's threat to "kick the god-damned soul" out of the much smaller and slightly built Kipling. After four years in America, total withdrawal seemed the only way out, so the Kipling family returned to England.

Back home Kipling told his friends: "There are only two places in the world where I want to live—Bombay and Brattleboro. And I can't live in either."

Naulakha was the Landmark Trust's first property in North America, which means you and up to seven other Kipling fans can rent it and stay where the great author himself once lived, and with all Kipling furniture intact, write at his desk and bathe in his tub. Up to eight guests may stay at Naulakha, which includes four bedrooms (three twin, one double); three bathrooms; full kitchen; washer, dryer and dishwasher. Dogs are allowed. All bookings must be made through the Office of the Landmark Trust USA.

Directions: The Kipling home is located north of Brattleboro, off I-91 at exit 3. Turn south on U.S. Route 5 at the traffic circle, right on Black Mountain Road, and right again on Kipling Road to #707.For rental information, call Office of the Landmark Trust, 802.254.6868, or visit www.landmarktrustusa.org;

YOUTUBE VIDEO:
"Rudyard Kipling's Jungle Book House In Vermont" (5:41)
(Interesting old-timey tour of Naulakha; many others available) ✤

THEY DON'T MAKE SENATORS LIKE GEORGE ANYMORE

Dummerston

George D. Aiken, born in Dummerston and educated in Putney and Brattleboro, was a maverick Republican Vermont U.S. senator for thirty-four years, from 1941 to 1975 and Vermont's governor for one term before that. Senator Mike Mansfield, a Democratic leader in the Senate during the time Aiken served, called him "the wise old owl" for his statement during the Vietnam War that we should declare victory and get out—a balance between the "hawks" who wanted victory at any cost, and the "doves" who wanted to withdraw at any cost.

Aiken wrote of a "Vermont with a heritage of ideals that included the principles of loving liberty, self-reliance, thrift, and liberalism." The senator practiced what he preached. As to thrift and self-reliance alone, in his last campaign for office at age seventy-five, he spent only $17. And this was only his second least expensive campaign. In 1956 he was able to get by on $1.08. If, as they say, money buys access, Senator George Aiken got significantly more than his money's worth, as did his constituents. ❦

PERCUSSION INSTRUMENTS TO THE STARS

Gageville (North Westminster)

Driving west on Route 121, about a mile out of Bellows Falls, you'll see a small sawmill on the left. From the outside the long, low buildings, stacks of lumber, forklifts, and cones of sawdust will remind you of most sawmills you've seen in your lifetime: men using machines to convert felled trees into planks, timbers, and milled wood pieces of various sizes and shapes.

But Cooperman is one of the last of what used to be known as "fife and drum companies." It still manufactures both drums and fifes—four models of rope-tension field drums and a dozen varieties of fifes alone. But it also produces what no other company in the world does: hundreds of bodhráns, tars, bendirs, hadjiras, ghavals, kanjiras, riqs, and pandeiros. "Huh?" you say. These happen to be custom-made hand drums that originated in North Africa, Morocco, India, Egypt, Persia, and Azerbaijan—all in high demand by percussionists and hand drummers throughout the jazz, folk, classical, and contemporary music worlds. (Paul Simon's percussionist Jamey Haddad designed the Cooperman hadjira, which actually is a twentieth-century adaptation of several existing drums from Egypt, Brazil, and south India.)

Master drum-maker (and vice president) Jim Ellis puts the finishing touches on a rope tension post-Civil War-style field drum at the Cooperman Fife and Drum Company.

"The drumheads are made from calfskin and goatskin—in the case of the riqs, from fish skin," says Patrick Cooperman, who heads the company. "The tannery for our only domestic head producer, in Sheboygan, Wisconsin, burned down a few years ago. Now we rely on tanneries in England, Germany, and Pakistan. Each has its own distinctive sound for different instruments."

"My father began building drums more than fifty years ago," says Patrick, "and started the company with my mother, who still works here." Actually, five members of the Cooperman family are employed by the company, which numbers just twenty-one men and women.

The 2,000–2,500 hardwood logs Cooperman goes through each year also result in sixty finished banjos and one hundred tambourines weekly. "We use only the butt log," says Patrick, "which is the first eight feet of the tree." The trees are all local hardwoods: poplar, cherry, ash, maple, and birch.

Every other wooden-instrument manufacturer has gone to laminated wood, but Cooperman alone forms its drum and string-instrument frames from wood bent by machine after it is steamed to optimum flexibility.

Does Paul Simon know his percussionist buys custom-made instruments from a little sawmill in rural Vermont? "If you asked him that question, I think he'd be dumbfounded," Patrick says.

Directions: For more information see www.cooperman.com or call (802) 463-9750.

YOUTUBE VIDEO:
"Tour of Cooperman Drum Factory" (2:31)
(Interesting message, but production values need help) 🍁

DAIRY FARM RESURRECTION

Grafton

Tulip (left) and Tootsy at rest after milking. Keltsey Rushton names all cows to neutralize any numbers-only identity.

From 1965 to 2015, the number of dairy farms in Vermont fell from more than 6,000 to fewer than 900. In Rockingham over that same period, they went from 50 to 0. Arnold Fisher, who owned the last dairy farm in town, sold his 50 cows in 2010. Arnold's

**No signage confirms this, but the Milk Shack opens a little after
3 a.m., just before Mark starts his morning chores.**

neighbor down the road and childhood friend Dick Stickney sold
his herd to son Pete four years earlier to stock the dairy farm Pete
now manages at Putney School. Dick maintains that estimates
regarding dairy industry freefall statewide were misleading, and
that because of larger herds and more diversification, Vermont's
dairy farmers in the state today were thriving.

"The Rushton Farm in Grafton," Dick told me, "does about
the best job around. First, they're in the top three or four percent
in the state as far as production per cow—both for protein and
for butterfat. They also get a better price based on their milk's low
raw bacteria count.

"Second, what a farmer does is important—but when he does it
is just as important. For example, Rushton makes sure he cuts his
crops on time, when they have their maximum nutritional value.
That's the key to good production. Third, they have a nutritionist
come in on a regular basis, to advise them on any changes that
should be made in the cows' feeding habits."

At the farm a couple of days later, Sue Rushton talked about farming with her husband Mark, and son and daughter Sam and Keltsey. They raise and care for 110 Holsteins and Jerseys, and twice a day milk 60 to 70 of them, on average. The total daily production averages 3,500 pounds (at about 8 pounds to the gallon).

The 70 Rushton milking cows are just half of Vermont's average of 140 cows per farm, but its diversity immediately identifies it as "thriving." The work involved, though, as I learned when Sue walked me through the farm's various activities, is monumental.

To begin with, in addition to the cows there are the chickens: 125 laying hens averaging one egg per day, and 100 broilers, sold retail when they reach full growth.

Next are the turkeys. Sue and Mark buy about 35 chicks a year in July, and sell them at Thanksgiving time, when their average weight is 25 pounds.

After that are the 20 pigs. And the bulls—three little ones (when I visited)—soon to be valuable breeders on someone else's farm. Sue's background as a former professional breeder makes her the obvious choice as artificial breeder of all the cows and heifers on the farm.

Last is the Rushtons' significant retail business. Mark buys wood by the truckload, and after cutting, splitting, and drying, sells it to customers in surrounding towns.

There's also hay for sale, round bales six feet in diameter wrapped in white plastic. And we can't forget "The Milk Shack," a year-round, unmanned, honor-system-based store, open at the very farm-like hours of 3:30 a.m. - 9 p.m.—selling raw milk, chicken eggs, frozen whole chickens, beef and pork, ice cream by the quart and single servings, cakes, and cookies baked by Mark's mother. About the ice cream: Twice monthly Sue drives to Temple, New Hampshire to pick up 28 gallons at a time. The Connolly Brother's Dairy supply the ice cream and will add anything Sue wants to create original flavors.

In the summer on weekends from 2 p.m. – 8 p.m., an outdoor drive-in called "The Scoop" sells Sue's ice cream as well. I can testify that the scoops are way over on the generous side. "I'll tell you when to stop," the fourteen-year-old proprietor instructs the ten-year-old he is teaching how to fill an order. (Most on the payroll are neighbor kids.)

After the week she puts in, Sue still has energy enough to put together a Sunday supper during the summer—on picnic tables and under a tent—for $5.00, the night we were there, consisting of scrumptious pulled pork, a homemade roll, and first-rate coleslaw.

On three holiday evenings—Memorial Day, July 4, and Labor Day—the Rushtons invite fiddlers to play for anyone interested; church members donate the drinks and hotdogs, and the Rushtons donate their time, their farm, and hamburgers for the event, with all proceeds going to the Grafton Church.

Now, how does all this get done by a family of four (in addition to the young Scoop staff)? After high school, Sam graduated from Vermont Technical College in 2016 with a major in dairy farm management and is now using his additional education back on the farm full-time. Keltsey is finishing up two years at Vermont Tech this year and will go on to UVM* as part of the state's 2+2 program, meaning that in two years she will graduate with a Bachelor of Science degree in dairy farm management. Mark, Sam, and Keltsey all volunteer for the Grafton Fire Dept.

So Mark is up at 3 a.m. and opens up the Milk Shack, among other duties. Sue sleeps in until 4:20 or so, with Keltsey joining her shortly thereafter (as her school schedule permits). Sam likes to sleep until summoned, but is up shortly thereafter and puts in hard work days beginning right after breakfast. By the way, Mark also helps out when he can on a 100-acre farm in Chester where his folks now live.

All of this, I'm thinking, will lead me to the phone first thing tomorrow: "Hello, Guinness? What's your current record for family multitasking?"

YOUTUBE VIDEO:
"Rushton Farm Storm Damage, Grafton, Vermont" (1:06)
(Rushton Farm did not escape 2012's tropical storm Irene—see Chapter 1) ❦

---

* "UVM" is both a nickname for the University of Vermont and an abbreviation of the Latin for University of the Green Mountains, *Universitas Viridis Montis.*

TASTE DELIGHTS FROM A SCHOOL BUS IN A MEADOW

Putney

**Just out of sight beyond the bus (right) Is the grill tended by Curtis,
where seven days a week, seven months a year, he works to justify
his "Ninth Wonder of the World" renown.**

If you drive into Curtis's Barbecue most any day between 10:00 a.m.
and dusk, look to the right. You'll see smoke curling above a meat
pit as rows of rising gray beams meet the sunshine. Right away you
know something special is afoot. The entrance sign reads: NINTH
WONDER OF THE WORLD. That sounds about right.

With a long-handled fork, Curtis Tuff deftly moves five-pound
slabs of pork ribs and half chickens to warmer or cooler spots on
his 5-foot-by-10-foot grill, depending on their degree of doneness.
Sleeping soundly next to that grill is C.J. (Curtis Jr.), his pet pig—
never, he swears, to be on the menu. Behind Curtis in this three-acre
meadow are two blue school buses where orders are filled, including

side dishes such as baked potatoes, coleslaw, corn on the cob, and baked beans. Says *Gourmet* magazine's roadside reporter Michael Stern: "The ribs are cooked so the meat pulls off in big, succulent strips that virtually burst with piggy flavor and the perfume of smoke." Both spicy and mild homemade sauces are at the ready.

In a state better known for cheese and maple syrup, ribs are about the last specialty food you'd expect to find. Yet Curtis has been at this site since 1968, going through twenty-one cords of hardwood or more every season (at least five of which he splits himself). He has put two daughters through Vermont Academy and Mount Ida College.

Directions: From I-91, take exit 4 and go north on U.S. Route 5 for less than half a mile. Curtis's Barbecue is on the right, just before the service station. Curtis's is open April through October, Thursday–Sunday, 10:00 a.m. to 7 p.m. For more information visit www.curtisbbqvt.com or call (802) 387-5474.

YOUTUBE VIDEO:
"This Is Vermont: Curtis BBQ, Putney, VT" (3:27)
A mini-documentary, narrated by Curtis ♣

L. L. B. ANGAS—"THE MAJOR"

Saxtons River

On April 9, 1935, New York newspaper financial pages ran the following boxed ad: "Major Lawrence Lee Bazley Angas, Investment Counsel, has taken an office at the Waldorf-Astoria. He respectfully solicits inquiries." This marked the arrival from England of a dashing, flamboyant, mustachioed Oxford University graduate who was a Wall Street force to be reckoned with for the next twenty years, and who for almost twenty years thereafter ran one of the most bizarre one-man entrepreneurial empires ever seen in Saxtons River, Vermont. Major Angas was drawn to the United States in the depths of the American Depression after writing a successful pamphlet for Simon & Schuster called *The Coming of the American Boom*. His accurate predictions earned him such clients as J.P. Morgan & Co.

**The Inn at Saxtons River, former residence of financier
Lawrence Lee Bazley Angas.**

and the United States Treasury. (His $200/hour consultation fee, converted from 1940 dollars, would be $3,400 today, and allowed him to care adequately for the wife and daughter he left in England.) The Major wore his rapidly accelerating wealth with style. He drove 12-cylinder Cadillac convertibles. His custom-tailored suits included inside pouch pockets for emergency quantities of 12-inch Havana cigars and copies of his *Angas Digests*. The refrigerator he installed in his Waldorf-Astoria suite always held enough champagne, hors d'oeuvres, gin, and vermouth to stock the impromptu parties he frequently hosted.

Saxtons River resident Humphrey Neill, another Wall Street guru during Angas's New York years, was destined to meet him and become friends because their personalities meshed so well. Neill was as much of an iconoclast as was the Major, and in 1954 convinced him to move to Saxtons River and leave the city's hustle and bustle to carry out his work in a quieter, more peaceful atmosphere.

Unfortunately, Major Angas brought more of his bombastic personality to Saxtons River than any peace and quiet he took from the community. An avid and excellent golfer, he often drove balls down the middle of Pleasant Street outside the first house he bought in the village—at midnight or later, in his underwear, after a hard day of writing. When confronted by a neighbor the morning after one such occasion, he said in shocked surprise: "You must be mistaken. What was I wearing?" When she reminded him, he replied: "You know, it's not proper for a young woman to spy on a man in his underwear."

After two years, the Major bought the Saxtons River Inn on Main Street—with its five-story tower, the largest building in town—and turned it into his personal home and office. All twenty-five of the guest rooms became receptacles for his growing quantities of books and files. The few friends and neighbors who were invited to visit for canned salmon and champagne said that even the large dining room and adjacent parlor were crammed with boxes, crowded shelves, and bookcases to the extent that it was almost impossible to navigate from room to room. A two-story side porch running the length of the inn was converted to a driving range—complete with a net to practice his swing—because the Major was writing the ultimate book on golf. He became even more reclusive but did find space in his Cadillac-strewn parking lot to create an ice rink for town youngsters. (He was also a first-rate skater and skier, and supposedly competed for England in the 1912 Olympics.)

The Major's death in 1973, two days before his 80th birthday, was as dramatic as his life had been. Late one evening, it is thought while in his third-floor bedroom warming himself in front of an electric heater, his bathrobe caught fire. He ran down the two flights of stairs and rolled in the snow to put out the blaze, but his burns were so severe that he died a few days after being taken to Bellows Falls Hospital. He is buried across the river in the town cemetery, next to his friend Humphrey Neill.

Saxtons River Cemetery is across the bridge, where both the Major and Humphrey Neill are buried, one block up the hill and on the left. See the "Grave Location Directory" just outside the cemetery. Humphrey Neill's house, still in the family, is three blocks west of the

Inn on Pleasant Valley Road, on the right just after Route 121 curves left. Visit www.innsaxtonsriver.com.

The Saxtons River Inn and Restaurant is easy to spot on Main Street in the center of town. Innkeeper and owner Sarah Campbell offers impeccable lodging, fine dinners, and a knowledge of the surroundings based on her life growing up in the area. To maximize your time here, in other words, Sarah is a go-to source. Also hosted at the Inn are weddings, other celebrations of life, and a wide range of community events. Incidentally, the Inn is one of several village epicenters of a Fourth of July day-long gala that attracts visitors from miles around. https://www.saxtonsriverinn.com. 802.869.2110. ❧

"BIG WIND AT ROCKINGHAM"

Rockingham Meeting House

On the hillside forgotten Puritans merge
with the earth beneath their splitting slate,
time-fractured markers cut with wigged faces
hearing wings, or children caught in alien sleep,
their young mothers remembered in a flourish
of lamentation, childbirth, and blood
all metered and rhymed in eighteenth-century grief.
The big wind rises, and loose snow lifts
and whirls around their stones, crumbling now
in the passage of centuries of changeless sorrow,
what hard wind slipped and hung round them
in the gallows of their cold thought?
This high, lean church, as unadorned
as their certain pride shadows down on them
in all the cold verses of their faith.
The great, waving bushes of the yard
shake, blossomless now, glittering in ice,
crackling in the wooing wind, whose drones
weave round the stalks like dreams
of wisping women, gowned and malign.
Or so these dead might have thought

courtesy of the author

had they stood among their stones
in this big wind over Rockingham,
where I stand among them looking out
at sweeping acres all snowed down
in the high cried winds that seem
a part of them, of their hard time
and of a set and shouldered faith.
And I think on their sculptors' dreams,
of all that winging of slate;
mere heads or heads and shoulders
or whole bodies angeling away
toward what austerity had promised,
or heaven like this cold blown hill
in Rockingham, little better
for a reward's sake, for a blessing,
from their final compact with the soil,
in this big wind over Rockingham.
I move to the margins of their yard
and stand looking out at those sweeping acres

all snowed, immaculate in the consolation
of winter, watching light fall warm on the white hills
far brighter than the angelic prayers,
the slate-cut hopes of sculptors, of elders,
and of their fragile, frightened children.

—John Wood
The Fictions of History

YouTube Video
"Meetinghouse in Rockingham, VT" (1:35)
(Interior, with window views of cemetery)

Also see Wikipedia entry for John A. Wood, Poet ❧

An Uncommonly Fatal Survey?

Saxtons River

Each year the organizers of Saxtons River's Fourth of July fes-
tivities prepare a program that includes the day's happenings, as
well as a short history of the village. The program is available to
everyone waiting to watch the traditional parade. "Traditional"
in this sense means quality valued over quantity. In years past,
for example, the relatively small procession ran through town
west to east, and then made a return pass east to west. The
program I read some years ago included the information that
Saxtons River—municipality as well as waterway—both were
named for surveyor Frederick Saxton. Unfortunately, Mr. Saxton
never experienced the glory that should have been afforded him.
While fixing the border between Westminster and Rockingham
townships, the luckless surveyor fell into the river and drowned.

But wait! A look at the 1859 *Gazetteer of Vermont* tells us that
"a Mr. Saxton . . . unluckily fell in while crossing [the river] on
a log but was not drowned.: And, writes Dr. Silvio Bedini in a
May-June 2004 *American Surveyor story*, "that particular surveyor
named Saxton has not been identified." Dr. Bedini concludes

that actually there were at least two surveyors named Frederick Saxton—father and son, it is presumed—and that both were reported to have drowned, "but neither was the Saxton for whom the river may have been named.

Hmmm.

But wait. As early as 1724, and before any surveys in the area had been made, the river already was known as Saxtons River. So might there have been a *third* Saxton, perhaps also named Frederick? And might he also have been a surveyor? This, writes Dr. Bedini, is the sole remaining mystery unsolved. Actually, I can think of one other, far less fanciful, for one thing—and certainly of more interest, particularly to you grammarians out there. Why is there no apostrophe after the "n" in "Saxtons"? It sure looks like a possessive to me. Show of hands, please—not that it will make any difference at this late date. Hey, I thought we were just enjoying ourselves here.

MAKING MINIMALIST SUGAR PRODUCTION WORK

Saxtons River

We'll let Tim tell this story himself.

"One Saturday morning in March last year, I was awakened by daughters Anna and Lia's cadenced cries: 'No maple syrup! No maple syrup!' As I drove to the market, I vowed this breakfast failure would never happen again. And from a single small dilemma, a maple-sugaring business was born.

"As founder, research and development fell to me. Then fate stepped in. Later that morning Dave Moore, local inn owner and paint contractor, pulled into our driveway with his two sons and a few dozen empty tin buckets in his pickup bed. Hearing my plan, Dave looked me straight in the eye. 'Four words,' he said. 'Tree selection is key.' We narrowed our search to the only sugar maple on our property. Its girth suggested to Dave that we had a three- or four-bucket specimen. I settled modestly for the three-bucket option. Our one-family, one-tree business could always expand.

courtesy of Tim Clark

Tim Clark's daughters Lia (foreground) and Anna helped their father by advising him to plow profits from last year back into capital investment, thus tripling this year's production to nine quarts.

"Over the next few days we assembled pots, pans, filter paper, candy thermometer, and jars from our kitchen, cellar, and the local general store: Then came the sap collection. We boiled it on the kitchen stove to evaporate the water; sampled and quality controlled the resulting syrup; and, finally, bottled and marketed our product. Along the way we learned about the sap-bucket drip rate, bug and debris filtration, and fuel-to-boiling-temperature ratio. These are among the technical issues that assaulted us those first few days.

"All start-up manufacturing ventures face critical viability moments. Either make the right call or fail. Our moment came when I noticed that using our soup pot to turn sap into syrup was going to take forever. Instead, I bought a large, shallow aluminum pan that covered two stove burners. We tripled our boil-time efficiency with that one move alone. At the end of the first week, we were enjoying our first homemade maple syrup.

"Looking back at that first production run, it seems amazing that we were able to produce anything remotely resembling syrup with our crude technology. The next season our technique and efficiency improved. Not only did we meet our family syrup needs, but neighbors and friends benefited as well. With new maple saplings sprouting in our backyard, we believe sweet success seems likely for generations to come." 🍁

PRE-NATAL TESTING BREAKTHROUGH

Saxtons River

Dee as a bridesmaid at her brother Jim's wedding.

When Dr. James Macri and wife Jane saw in 1971 that Deanne, their first child, had been born with a condition called spina bifida, Jim's immediate instinct was to do anything he could to both learn the cause of this defect and how to cure it. As it happened, nobody alive was better suited for the challenge.

Jim Macri graduated from Long Island University in 1965 with a major in biology, and five years later earned a Ph.D. in

Basic Medical Science. But while puzzling over the reasons for and causes of Deanne's spina bifida (meaning her spinal column hadn't closed completely while it was developing before she was born), no one—including the experts—was able to answer his questions. In that precise instant Jim completely changed the focus of his research to bio-chemical genetics, which required a considerable amount of new learning.

The Dee Run embodies the challenges Dee faced head-on, which the foundation in her name offers help to applicable and welcoming communities. You can't help wishing you knew her.

"My first thought, coming in as I did with a blank slate, was there's *got* to be a way to address this," Jim recalled. "I had no preconceived notions, which was good. On the other hand, when I dug a little deeper, asking questions like 'Why did this happen?' Nobody had any idea. 'When does it happen?' No idea.

"When I began looking into the problem, it quickly became clear that spina bifida occurs at a stage of pregnancy where neither the mother nor her physician knows she's pregnant. It takes place between days 28 and 30. That is also the precise time at which the central nervous system is forming and developing. When there is a fundamental failure in one spot or another in that development, you're left with spina bifida, also called 'neural tube defect.' If it develops in the brain it becomes a lethal issue. If it occurs anywhere along the spinal cord, it's variable: The lower and farther away from the brain, the better; the higher and closer, the worse."

But Jim had to find out for himself. By developing a procedure to take fluid from around the fetus, he was able to tell with nearly 100 percent certainty whether spina bifida was or was not a factor. This was a Eureka moment. He knew now he was on the right track. In 1974, he assembled a team to share the workload, and two years later he started Neural Tube Defect (NTD) Labs, which eventually made it possible to provide pre-natal screening to women of all ages as early as the first trimester of pregnancy.

In these same five years, meanwhile, Dee was growing into a happy, intellectually curious girl in her Long Island, New York hometown of Oyster Bay. Her sister Sarah was a year old, and though the testing procedures her father had invented were not yet available to her mother, Sarah was born healthy—as were her brother Jim and sister Elizabeth a few years later.

The following year, Dee entered first grade in Theodore Roosevelt Elementary School, and except for her leg braces and time away from school for various surgeries, was treated like every other pupil. She couldn't run well, for example, but nevertheless pitched on a recreational softball team. In one dancing scene in a high school play, the director choreographed Dee's "steps" to be with her arms—which she performed behind a sofa. "She spent her whole life attempting to function and perform as if she really didn't have a deficiency," says Jim.

From the age of five, Dee treated her spina bifida almost like an enemy she must know well enough to defeat and peppered her dad with questions about each operation. "She even knew their medical names," says Jim. "Imagine being in fifth grade and able to talk about a "derotational osteotomy!" Her personality was such that she maintained lifelong relationships with doctors and clinicians well beyond their professional dealings. Her sharp sense of humor also served her well. Dee selected her major at Long Island University to help her prepare children and young adults to succeed. She organized groups in after-school activities, and supervised programs to help men and women get the high school diplomas they had failed to earn earlier.

In 1998, Jim and Jane bought a cabin in Saxtons River, near Jane's hometown of Chester, and began coming up on weekends to work on it. Dee stayed in Oyster Bay meantime, in an apartment in the family home.

In 2006, Jim sold NTD Labs after making ground-breaking contributions to early screening for spina bifida (also for Down syndrome). More than 100 patents are registered in his name for a variety of discoveries. Thanks to this groundwork, highly specialized surgeons across the U.S. now perform fetal surgery on spina bifida babies on a regular basis, stitching their spines before they are born.

In 2013, Dee was in Saxtons River with her parents, on the mend and in physical therapy from a procedure performed just weeks earlier and was looking forward to moving into her own place in Norwood, Massachusetts. Sarah lived nearby, and Jim and Jane had outfitted the first floor of the house to accommodate her disability, no matter how severe it might become.

But this was not to be. Dee died, unexpectedly and in her sleep, on June 16, 2013. "It was a complete surprise when she went," Jane recalls. "She was on the mend, and we still don't completely understand what happened. Still, I remember her youngest sister saying after the service: 'Dee, your life will embrace us forever.'"

The following year, Jim and Jane renovated the entire house in Norwood to accommodate the physically challenged. Five residents have lived there since 2015.

Months later, the Macris created The Dee Foundation, which now assists dozens of communities and organizations that create projects embracing all of their citizens and members. Information about Foundation grants and events can be found at www.thedeefoundation.org. One of the most prominent events is The Dee Run, a 5K race scheduled every October. ✤

STRATTON MOUNTAIN: WORLD HEADQUARTERS FOR SNOWBOARDING

Stratton Village

**Another fun day of snowboarding where it all began—
Stratton Mountain, Vermont.**

Most people agree that the sport of snowboarding began in the eastern half of the United States, specifically in Vermont. There are claims from the Mount Baker area of Washington, and even from Breckenridge, Massachusetts, but Stratton Mountain, near Bondville, gets most of the votes. Stratton Mountain has been home to the U.S. Open Snowboarding Championships for more than twenty years and opened its lifts and trails to snowboarding in 1983.

When snowboarding pioneer Bud Keene was asked by *Vermont Sports Online* why Vermont has produced so many outstanding snowboarders, he said: "There are more halfpipes along Route 100 than in most other places in the U.S. And then there's the eastern mindset—riding in bad weather, in adverse conditions, riding on ice. . . . Tradition also plays a role. This is the birth of snowboarding and it makes for a small ecosystem back here."

Stratton Mountain Resort is located on the highest peak in southern Vermont, 20 miles from Manchester. It is the largest resort in the region. If you visit, a twelve-passenger gondola will take you from the resort to the peak of 3,936-foot Stratton Mountain.

Directions: From 1-91, take exit 2, and then on Route 30 drive approximately 30 miles north to Bondville. Stratton Mountain Resort is 4 miles from Bondville. For more information visit www.stratton.com, which tells not only about the resort but also about the surrounding area, or call (800) 787-2886.

YouTube Video:
"Flash Mob: World Snowboard Day 2012, Stratton Mountain Resort" 1:06)
"U.S. Open Snowboarding Championships - Live from Stratton Mountain Resort, VT" (3:03) ❦

SLOWING DOWN? NO WAY

Townshend

When I dropped in on Warren Patrick not long ago, he was at his typewriter working on "Shades of Grey," an autobiographical version of the popular novel and movie, "Fifty Shades of Grey." I looked over his shoulder at the opening lines, in which were recounted one of his earliest experiences with the opposite sex.

First though, you should know that Warren's home for the past ten years has been an independent living apartment at West Valley Senior Housing, in Townshend. The day I visited him was a week before his 107th birthday. Warren reminisced a bit, tongue firmly in cheek. "Last year we had a fire extinguisher ready when they lit my cake. This year we may need a fire permit—and maybe a bigger cake."

Before Warren moved to West Valley he lived in Jamaica (Vermont, that is), where he and his wife raised three daughters. "Three daughters now in their 70s and 80s. Can you imagine?" Over the years he worked as a farmer, carpenter, aircraft engine assembler during World War II—and later ran his own real estate

61

Sally Wadsworth

Warren's writing output includes a children's book, several newspaper articles, and an anecdote on pages 9-10 of *Vermont . . . Who Knew?*

and insurance businesses. After his wife died in 1994 and his daughters married and moved away, Warren lived alone until he was 97, and then "my daughters took my car keys away and told me I had to move one more time. I haven't regretted one minute here, though. The people are great, and I pretty much do as I please, as long as I behave myself." The only prescribed medicine he takes is a blood thinner. He pauses, and then says: "Although I did lose a tooth last month."

Warren goes to bed every evening at ten and is up next morning at seven. Until a year or so ago he began his day with a series of leg exercises, lying on his bed and lifting them back over his head and against the wall three times—occasionally (as happened when I was there on one occasion) shaking the framed pictures above his headboard. He then lifts weights for ten minutes. After breakfast he walks around the building and then into the woods for a half mile or so. His only vice: an occasional Budweiser.

But back to "Shades of Grey"; circa 1925, when Warren was a freshman in high school. His first paragraph went as follows:

"At the age of 107, I think I'm qualified to write my thoughts on this subject. The following will certainly interest you, provoke a few chuckles, and perhaps even a tear." From this low-key opening, the story could go almost anywhere, but I've made an executive decision: We'll wait for the finished work to appear rather than judge it based on the sliver Warren has written so far.

I didn't get through a complete description of Warren's typical day, but here is part of a letter he sent me before I next saw him. "In answer to your question, in my spare time I do many things. I start the day and end it with a prayer. I read the newspaper and sometimes write an article. One appeared a few days ago in a local newspaper and had to do with how many towns and cities on the east coast got their names from the colonists—for example, New York, New Britain, and New Bedford.

"I read several magazines and subscribe to *Time.* I watch the Red Sox and the Patriots ("I can't believe Tom Brady was guilty in 'Deflategate'! With his hand size, what would have been the advantage?), do crossword puzzles, and joke with the staff. I'm the oldest resident at 107, and the most active by far. We have an elevator, but I mostly use the stairs. I often cook for myself and share with other residents. I'm fully in agreement with 'Use it or lose it.' My only advice would be: 'Keep active and keep occupied.'"

When I visited him again the following week, he told me, "Last weekend I was a guest at two birthday parties—one here and one with many family members." That second, of course, would be his 107th, about which he added lightly, "It's only a number."

Warren's farewell request when we said goodbye: "If you find that tooth between here and the front door, let me know." (Cue rim shot.)

For more information about Warren's home, see www.valleycares.org (and click the "Contact Us" page for an unexpected testimonial). 🍁

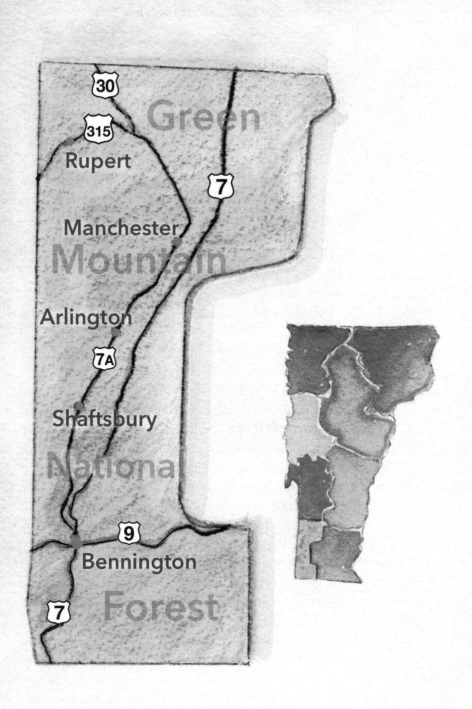

Southwest Region

3
SOUTHWEST

At present, I am living in Vermont.

—Robert Frost (from his poem "New Hampshire")

Early in this chapter you'll learn about two artistic mysteries and how they were solved. The first had to do with one of Norman Rockwell's most famous paintings. A copy of it masquerading as the real article fooled hundreds of thousands of museum visitors all over the world for more than forty years before a sharp-eyed viewer blew the whistle in 2002. The guilty replicator? One of Rockwell's dearest friends. Less than 20 miles south, on U.S. Route 7.A little over a decade earlier, Bennington Museum curators waited in vain for a shipment of Grandma Moses, paintings bequeathed by a recently deceased Pennsylvania florist and friend of the painter. Fourteen years later, the paintings arrived in two wooden crates addressed to the museum director. The only clue to their whereabouts? A cryptic note on purple mimeograph paper inside one of the crates.

Now who would have pegged Abraham Lincoln's eldest son as a zealous golfer and captain of industry? But that's what he became. And years after a number of summers in Vermont with his mother and brother (his dad wasn't able to take that much time off), Robert Todd Lincoln built a twenty-four-room house in Manchester for his wife and three children. But it was one of his granddaughters who showed a spirit reminiscent of Abe himself. Mary Lincoln Peggy Beckwith became known as the "Amelia Earhart of Vermont," routinely landing one of her three planes in a meadow near the house. Peggy was also an artist, photographer, guitarist, fencer, and cross-country skier. After three generations, you might say, the apple rolled back somewhat closer to the tree.

THE COUNTERFEIT NORMAN ROCKWELL— A MYSTERY

Arlington

courtesy of Don Trachte Jr.

Moments before this photo was taken in 2006, brothers Don and Dave Trachte discovered the original Rockwell "Breaking Home Ties" painting In their Dad's Arlington studio.

Do any of you older-timers remember a Norman Rockwell painting—first seen on the cover of a 1954 issue of the *Saturday Evening Post*—depicting a boy waiting with his dad and his dog for the train taking him off to college for the first time? Even if so, you probably don't remember the title: It was *Breaking Home Ties.* The boy looks eagerly down the road. His rancher father, in denim and boots, sits resignedly beside him on the running board of their truck, holding his hat in his hands. They have said all there is to say. The family collie, head in its master's lap, is disconsolate. The image remains the second most popular cover in the magazine's history. (First was "Saying Grace," a 1951 cover also painted by Rockwell.

In 1960, comic strip illustrator and artist Donald Trachte, a longtime friend and neighbor of Rockwell's in Arlington, bought *Breaking Home Ties* for $900 at a Southern Vermont Art Center exhibition of Rockwell's work. It remained one of his most prized possessions. Ten years later, when Trachte and his wife divorced, that painting was part of a collection of eight that was given to the children. The parents, though, were awarded temporary custody of the paintings in their respective homes. Trachte chose the Rockwell, among several others, and hung it over his grand piano when it wasn't on loan to museums all over the world from Cairo to Moscow. His ex-wife kept five of the other paintings in the collection. For the next forty years, dealers and collectors pursued Trachte and his four children about purchasing *Breaking Home Ties*.

When Trachte moved into an assisted-living home in 2002, the children transferred what they thought was the original to the Rockwell Museum, in Stockbridge, Massachusetts. Over the next three years, *Breaking Home Ties* was seen by hundreds of thousands of visitors to the museum.

Before it was exhibited, a preparatory cleaning revealed several small discrepancies from the original *Saturday Evening Post* cover tear sheet. Curators concluded that these were the effects of time and travel, however, rather than chicanery. Even so, in 2004, one expert called it "a third-rate replica."

"Wow," Dave Trachte remembers thinking at the time, "our one and only treasure and people think it's no good."

Then, in 2005, Don Trachte died, giving his four children total access to their dad's home and studio. Two months later, when all four children visited the studio just after their dad's memorial service, Don Jr. found two nearly identical versions of a George Hughes painting in the closet of the studio.

"So now we have two clues," says Don, "suspicions of a fake Rockwell and the duplicate George Hughes paintings. We suspected something, but we just weren't putting two-and-two together."

In January of 2006 Don got a call from a New York gallery again questioning the authenticity of the Rockwell painting. After driving to Stockbridge for another look at *Breaking Home Ties*, Don and Dave agreed that there were subtle differences in the boy's face between the painting and their photo of the original. A restoration expert found no indication that the painting had been altered, but Dave was still skeptical. In March, looking through the studio yet again, he noticed a gap in the paneling of a wall next to an inset bookcase. He was able to push it enough to reveal the edges of several small paintings and quickly called Don in Burlington. Don arrived the next day with "deconstruction tools," but Dave's smile told him they wouldn't be needed. He had discovered that the panel slid easily. Out appeared several original paintings, copies of which their mother had hung on her walls. They moved to a second panel. Slowly, the edge of a larger painting became visible. First they saw a dog's tail, then the truck, then the boy. The original *Breaking Home Ties!*

The Trachte children believe that their father's underlying motive was to protect the family inheritance. "I'm not surprised," said their mother when the boys told her the story.

The original, in mint condition after its forty-year rest behind a wall (as opposed to the Trachte version's wear and tear of several hundred thousand travel miles), was sold at Sotheby's in New York for $15.4 million. The Trachte version and other paintings in that collection are on display from time to time at various museums. Both Sotheby's and the Rockwell Museum remain mum about the location of the original *Breaking Home Ties*. No surprise, really.

YouTube Videos
"Norman Rockwell" (7:16)
(A parade of Rockwell's *Saturday Evening Post* covers, musically accompanied, and including "Breaking Home Ties") ♣

Moonlight in Vermont

The classic and haunting ballad "Moonlight in Vermont" was written by two non-Vermonters. John Blackburn, who wrote the lyrics, taught drama for two years at Bennington College. He teamed with composer Karl Suessdorf when both worked in Los Angeles during World War II.

Composer Johnny Mercer liked the melody and brought it to vocalist Margaret Whiting in 1945. It created little splash, but when Whiting rerecorded the song ten years later, it made the top ten. It was subsequently recorded by such artists as Frank Sinatra, Ella Fitzgerald, Billie Holliday, Ray Charles, and Willie Nelson. In 1985 Vermont's legislature decreed a "Moonlight in Vermont Day," and Whiting made her first trip to the state to sing the song before a joint session of the legislature.

In the late 1990s this same legislature rejected "Moonlight in Vermont" as the official state song, partly, it was said, because it was too difficult for the average person to sing.

THE GRANDMA MOSES MUSEUM HEIST

Bennington

Here's how it went down: Anna Mary Robertson Moses began to paint seriously at age seventy-six, and in 1939 a New York art collector saw samples of her work displayed in a Hoosick Falls, New York, drugstore, 5 miles from her home in Eagle Bridge. This led to a one-woman show in 1940 and established Grandma Moses, as she was called, as a fixture in the history of American art.

Margaret Carr and Ruth Garner, sisters who ran a florist shop in Rose Valley, Pennsylvania, just outside Philadelphia, met Grandma Moses in 1952. They loved her work. Over the next few years, they paid her several visits, usually buying one or more paintings, either by the artist herself or by her son, Forrest King Moses. Eventually they became friends, talking by phone twice a year, sending gifts, and occasionally visiting Grandma Moses at her home in Eagle Bridge, where she occasionally gave them a painting they admired.

**In 1972, the New York schoolhouse attended by Grandma Moses
was moved to the Bennington Museum. It explores her work.**

On December 13, 1961, Grandma Moses died at the age of
101. She left her sister-friends a sofa and other memorabilia to
commemorate their friendship. When Margaret Carr died in 1984,
she bequeathed seven of the artist's paintings to the Bennington
Museum, plus the sofa, letters, clippings, and other gifts they had
received over the years.

Mrs. Carr had made meticulous arrangements to ship the
paintings and other materials to the museum. So far as the museum
knew, the shipment was on its way, but it never arrived. At different
times investigators from the Pennsylvania State Police, the FBI, and
the Galerie St. Etienne in New York City all went to Mrs. Carr's
home in Rose Valley and found the two Forrest Moses paintings,
the sofa, and memorabilia. The seven Grandma Moses paintings
had disappeared. All leads in the case dead-ended right there, and
that's how the matter stood for the next fourteen years.

Curator Jamie Franklin filled in the story from there. "On
February 9, 1998, the seven paintings arrived at the Bennington
Museum in two wooden crates addressed to Director Steve
Miller from a commercial shipping company in Quakerstown,

Pennsylvania," said Franklin. "A cryptic note on purple mimeograph paper was signed 'Ring Sar,' and attempts to trace the source of both the shipment and the shippers were unsuccessful."

All of the information the shippers provided the shipping company turned out to be false. Best guess is that the heist was perpetrated by a person or persons who had known Margaret Carr, as well as about the will, including the paintings' final destination. Because the paintings were kept in excellent condition and no paper trail exists that attempts were made to sell them over the fourteen years, a further guess is that the thieves were not interested in making a profit, but simply enjoyed the artist's work. A clean getaway!

The Bennington Museum holds the largest collection of art by Grandma Moses. Great-grandson Will Moses is continuing the family folk art tradition at the Mt. Nebo Gallery, in Eagle Bridge, New York.

Directions: The Bennington Museum is in downtown Bennington at 75 Main Street (Route 9). The museum is open daily, 10:00 a.m. to 5:00 p.m., through October. See www.benningtonmuseum.org for the best information, or call (802) 447-1571.

YOUTUBE VIDEO:
"Women Artists: Grandma Moses (4:57) 🍁

WHEN YOU DON'T WANT TO SETTLE FOR A ROLLS-ROYCE

Between 1920 and 1924 only eighteen Martin-Wasps were produced. Now this was the motor car to consider if a Pierce-Arrow or a Rolls-Royce wasn't exclusive enough for you. Karl H. Martin, a successful automobile coachwork designer for a number of New York companies, wanted to design and market an auto of his own. He went back to his hometown of Bennington, leased part of a foundry, and, with the help of a couple of financial backers, founded the Martin-Wasp Corporation.

Martin put twenty-eight people on his payroll, most of whom built the chassis of the Wasp by hand. All of his early models featured twin spare tires and a Saint Christopher's medal embedded in the dashboard. Martin created several body styles but priced them all at $10,000, which comes to just under $113,000 in today's dollars. At the New York Auto Show in 1920, screen star Douglas Fairbanks Jr. (who was first to leave footprints in wet cement outside Hollywood's Grauman's Chinese Theatre) bought a Wasp from Martin. But in 1924 one of Martin's principal backers died, and he closed down production.

Today the sole remaining Martin-Wasp is on display at the Bennington Museum. It was totally restored in the 1960s and still looks pretty spiffy with its dark green body and maroon wheels. I wasn't able to get an answer as to whether it could still maintain its original top speed of 15 miles per hour.

THE ONE, THE ONLY COVERED BRIDGE MUSEUM

Bennington

Just reading from the promotion here: "Discover the exciting history, culture, nature, science, and art of covered bridges in the first and only museum dedicated to the preservation of these wonderful structures."

First, I'm inclined to give them, but *only*? That might be a stretch. But then I think: A covered bridge that itself is a covered bridge museum, even if it is a reproduction . . . maybe we do have ourselves an "only."

It is a magical experience to go across a covered bridge for the first time, especially if you take a few minutes to examine the level of craftsmanship that went into its construction. The Vermont Covered Bridge Museum gives you an opportunity for this and provides 3-D models, dioramas, and a working covered bridge railroad layout to show in realistic detail what these bridges could do and how they did it. You can even sit at one of two computer workstations to build and test your own covered bridge design.

The Covered Bridge Museum is an exact replica of a town lattice bridge. It is connected—psychically and physically—to the Bennington Center for the Natural and Cultural Arts

The original purpose of the covered bridge was not to keep travelers from nasty weather. Its enclosing roof protected the timbers from weathering, which prolonged the life of the bridge. Nevertheless, this natural shelter was also used as a gathering place or picnic location. Covered bridges also were considered to be great boxing rings. It is said that Norwich University moved from Norwich to Northfield, Vermont, in an attempt to stop boxing matches on the Ledyard Bridge between its students and those of Dartmouth College.

Here's the skinny on the cost of crossing a Vermont river in the 1800s, when a covered bridge was between you and the other side ("A brief darkness leading from the light to light," as Henry Wadsworth Longfellow put it a bit more lyrically):

1800s COVERED BRIDGE BILL OF FARE

A man on foot	1 cent
A man on horseback	4 cents
A one-horse carriage	10 cents
A carriage drawn by more than one horse	20 cents
Cattle	1 cent (driver free)
Sheep or swine	½ cent (driver free)

Directions: The Vermont Covered Bridge Museum is located at 44 Gypsy Lane at Route 9 in Bennington and is part of the Bennington Center for the Arts. The museum is open 10:00 a.m.–5:00 p.m., Wednesday–Monday.(Tuesdays closed.) Check out www.benningtoncenterforthearts.org/vtCBM/ for a wide variety of information, or call (802) 442-7158. ❦

SHIRLEY JACKSON DAY

Bennington

Remember Shirley Jackson's "The Lottery," a chilling short story—and required reading in high school English classes for a half century?

In 2015, Random House released a collection of Jackson's unpublished short stories and essays called *Let Me Tell You.* This, plus a biography by Ruth Franklin and the reissue of *Raising Demons* and *Life Among the Savages*, her two hilarious novels about raising a family in Bennington, signal that Shirley Jackson's work is enjoying a revival.

North Bennington, where Jackson lived with her husband Stanley Hyman, is part of that renewed interest in her work. For the past several years the Left Bank, a community meeting place, has hosted an evening—usually in June—of readings and discussion about the famous author. It is said that her family members, some of whom still live in the area, often attend as well. Call 802.681.7161, or email Christine Graham at cpgraham@sovernet.com for details.

WOULD ABE LINCOLN HAVE SLEPT HERE?

Manchester

Today the home and grounds of Robert Lincoln serve as hub for activities such as children's camps, craft festivals, art shows, fairs, and concerts.

There's no way to break this other than just come right out with it: Abraham Lincoln's oldest son was a passionate golfer and a corporate titan. It seems the apple fell a good distance from the tree.

Most think this all started when Lincoln enrolled Robert at Harvard in 1861, the same year he took office as president. After his father's death Robert Todd Lincoln parlayed an inheritance of $110,000 or so (about $1.75 million in today's dollars), his name, and a law degree into a position as special counsel for the Pullman Corporation. In 1901, after George Pullman died, Lincoln was named president of the company. In less than a decade, he took Pullman from a $300,000 company to a $10 million company. (That's the "corporate titan" part.)

Robert Lincoln also served as secretary of war under presidents James Garfield and Chester A. Arthur, and as ambassador to the

United Kingdom under President Benjamin Harrison. Retiring in 1922, he made his last public appearance in Washington, D.C., in that same year for the dedication ceremony for his father's memorial.

Robert's love for the Manchester area began back in 1863, while his dad was president. That summer, as well as the following year, his mother, his brother, Tad, and he stayed at the Equinox Hotel, which still displays a copy of the guestbook page on which Mary Todd Lincoln registered. Mrs. Lincoln booked the entire family for the summer of 1865, a trip that the president did not live to take. In 1905, after spending more and more time in Manchester during the summers, Robert, his wife, and their three children moved into a twenty-four-room mansion they had built on 500 acres of land in the Battenkill Valley, smack-dab between Vermont's Green Mountains and the Taconic Range in New York. Robert's wife, Mary Harlan, named the house Hildene, an amalgam of two Old English words that together mean "hill and valley." The expansive front yard made a great driving range, where Robert was able to polish his long game between matches at the local country club. (That's the "passionate golfer" part.)

Of their three children Abraham "Jack" Lincoln II died at sixteen of blood poisoning. Because the other two children were girls, this ended the family name, but not the line of descendants. Daughter Jessie Harlan Lincoln married three times and produced a son and a daughter. The daughter, Mary Lincoln "Peggy" Beckwith, called Hildene home her whole life. The following paragraphs were written from notes taken during a conversation with Gary Sloan, a leading Hildene interpreter.

Peggy remained single and childless, perhaps leery of the experiences of both her mother and her brother, who married six times between them. But she did manage to cram a lot of living into her time at Hildene. She was a serious farmer and raised Black Angus cattle and dairy herds on the property. At times she kept several dogs and cats and adopted a couple of baby raccoons.

But she also had a passion as strong as her grandfather Robert's was for the game of golf: Peggy loved mechanized vehicles. She is said to have gone through several cars a year—sometimes buying back those she sold, after realizing she missed them so much she couldn't part with them.

Her reputation as the "Amelia Earhart of Vermont," was even more prominent. Between 1928 and 1933 Peggy owned as many as three single-engine two-place planes, taking off and landing from an airfield on the meadows by the farm. Her grandmother, Robert Todd's widow, was violently opposed to her granddaughter flying around in "one of those machines." Peggy convinced her grandmother to agree to a test: Peggy would land her plane in the front yard and prove that this was a safe and proper hobby, and that she (Peggy) was not in grave danger. But apparently Peggy failed the test. She landed safely but was unable to make a case good enough to change her grandmother's mind. That was the last of the flying in and about Hildene.

But Peggy remained a well-known figure about town and looked like anything but a millionaire, her in-town outfit usually consisting of overalls and boots. Children loved her, though, and sons and daughters of staff members could be found weekends watching *Howdy Doody* or the *Beverly Hillbillies* around her television set— one of the few to be found In town. When the kids got thirsty, there was a Coke machine nearby.

Mary Lincoln Peggy Beckwith was also an artist and an accomplished photographer. She fenced, she loved cross-country skiing, she played guitar, and she composed for the piano. You have to believe she would have been a source of delight to her great-granddad.

Directions: On U.S. Route 7, take exit 3 (Route 313) toward Arlington. Turn right on Vermont Route 7A. Travel north for about 8 miles, and turn right onto Hildene Road. Hildene is open daily 9:30 a.m. to 4:30 p.m.(except for Thanksgiving, December 24, 25, 26, and Easter. (Don't miss the restored Pullman car exhibit, about a quarter-mile from the main house. It was the corporate jet of its day.) For more information visit www.hildene.org or call the Friends of Hildene at (802) 362-1788.

YOUTUBE VIDEO:
"Restored Pullman Car at Hildene" (2:33) ✤

BOOTH SAVES LINCOLN

In 1863 or 1864 (accounts vary), Harvard student Robert Lincoln was at a train station in Jersey City, New Jersey on a trip from New York to Washington, D.C. As he waited on a platform with other passengers to buy sleeper car tickets from a conductor, a growing crowd pressed him against the car in front of him. When the train started to move he was twisted off his feet and fell into the open space between the platform and the car. "I was helpless," Lincoln recalled in 1909, "but suddenly my coat collar was seized vigorously and I was pulled up to secure footing on the platform.

"Upon turning to thank my rescuer, I saw it was Edwin Booth [a famous Shakespearean actor of the day], whose face was of course well known to me. I expressed my gratitude to him, and in doing so called him by name." Booth, on the other hand, did not know whom he had saved until months later. Best estimates are that it was within a year that Edwin's brother, John Wilkes Booth, assassinated President Abraham Lincoln at Ford's Theatre on April 14, 1865. Robert Lincoln had talked to his father that day, but decided not to see the play with his parents that evening. After a twelve-day search, Booth was found, shot, and killed in a Virginia barn.

"I HAD A LOVER'S QUARREL WITH THE WORLD"

Shaftsbury

Robert Frost's headstone inscription succinctly summarizes the great disparity between his professional successes and personal tragedies over a lifetime of nearly eighty-nine years. His first moneymaking poem was published when he was twenty, he was the first writer to be awarded four Pulitzer Prizes, he lectured internationally, and in 1961 the Vermont legislature named him the poet laureate of Vermont.

Robert Frost moved from New Hampshire to Vermont In 1920. One reason: On the eighty acres of farmland, he could grow "a thousand apple trees of some unforbidden variety."

On the other hand, Frost's father died when the poet was eleven (leaving the family with $8 after expenses were paid), Frost's first son died at age four (and his mother four months later), his fourth daughter died after three days, his sister was committed to an insane asylum and later died there, his third daughter died shortly after her first daughter was born, and his second son committed suicide.

Although Frost is described as a Vermont poet, he was born in San Francisco, lived in Massachusetts until age twelve, finished high school in New Hampshire (as co-valedictorian of his class), lived in New Hampshire and Massachusetts after he was married, and moved to London with his wife and four remaining children for two years, where he published his first book of poetry; but then he moved back to Massachusetts again and then Michigan and finally, when he was fifty-five, to Shaftsbury, Vermont.

The Robert Frost Stone House Museum in Shaftsbury contains galleries in the house where Frost both lived and wrote some of his best poetry. One of his most famous poems, "Stopping by Woods on a Snowy Evening," was composed on a sweltering June morning at his dining room table. Other Stone House exhibits include the J. J. Lankes Gallery, featuring woodcuts of Frost's favorite illustrator, and the bookshop offering books, recordings, and posters. Frost's grave is located nearby in Old Bennington.

Directions: From Main Street in Bennington, go north on U.S. Route 7 to exit 2, Shaftsbury. At end of ramp, turn right onto Vermont Route 7A and go north. Go 3/4 mile past Hiland Hall School. The museum is on the left side, at 121 Historic Route 7A. The Stone House Museum is open from May 1 to October 31, 10:00 a.m.–5:00 p.m., Wednesday–Sunday. Admission; no credit cards. For more information visit www.frostfriends.org or call (802) 447-6200. ❧

ICE-FISHING CENTRAL

As long as there's been a Vermont, there's been ice fishing. According to the Ice Fishing Chat Forum, Michigan and Vermont attract the most North American icefishianados, followed closely by Maine.

Though most anglers store their fishing gear for the winter, more and more start cutting holes in the ice as soon as it's safe to walk on.

Every February for the past thirty-five years, the Deerfield Valley Sportsmen's Club has sponsored the Harriman Reservoir Ice Fishing Derby, one of dozens around the state. The first time they put this derby together, in 1985, it attracted 223 fishermen, fisherwomen, and fisherkids These days the event averages more than 800 participants and stretches over two days.

In addition to Harriman's ample fish population, the reservoir is stocked each year with 150 tagged brook trout(as well as the rainbows and browns of the species), plus a slew of perch and small- and large-mouth bass.

Catching the most-wanted tagged fish entitles the lucky angler to a $25,000 pickup truck. Total cash prizes average more than $60,000.

Families who fish continuously over the two-day period usually set up shanties. Those not barbecuing moose, bear, or other delicacies, can buy snacks and baked goods at stands run by high school students.

"We start soliciting the big sponsors in June," said Debra Cox, derby organizer at the time. "If you wait any later, the companies don't have any advertising money left when it's time to fine-tune schedules. We distribute papers all over the state, plus in New Hampshire, Massachusetts, and New York."

It could have been one of these papers that reached three young men in Massachusetts, who one year sent in registration fees and arrived at the Harriman with a few 36-inch farm-raised salmon in their cooler, which they had netted well before crossing the Vermont border. "We'd never seen fish like that in this lake," Debra said. A biologist assigned to the derby ended up proving it, because hatchery-raised fish contain implanted identifiers in their dorsal fins. They were also pretty well banged up from being contained in breeding tanks. "We contacted U.S. Fish and Wildlife, because the fish had been taken over state lines and submitted as legitimate contest entries here. They were hit with federal fines, as well. I doubt they'll be back again."

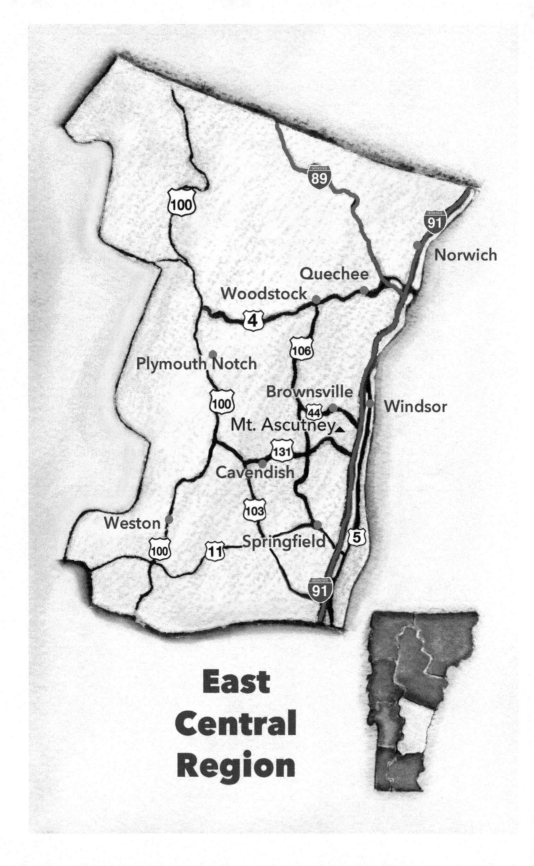

100

INTERSTATE
89

INTERSTATE
91

Norwich

Quechee
Woodstock

4

106

Plymouth Notch

100

Brownsville

44

Windsor

Mt. Ascutney▲

131

Cavendish

103

Weston

100

11

Springfield

5

INTERSTATE
91

East
Central
Region

4

EAST CENTRAL

Let's start with Phineas Gage, a hardworking railroad foreman. One day in 1846, while setting dynamite charges to blast rock from the route of a track-construction project near Cavendish, Gage was distracted by a fellow worker and rammed his thirteen-pound tamping rod directly onto the dynamite stick—before the hole had been filled with a protective sand cover. The resulting blast knocked the rod back up through Gage's cheekbone and out the top of his skull. And that's when his new life began. On the other side of Cavendish and well into the next century, recently exiled Soviet writer Aleksandr Solzhenitsyn was starting a new life in Vermont with his wife and three boys—with quite mixed results, as you'll see.

For a change of pace, learn about a telescope club so exclusive that to become a member you not only have to know all the constellations and how to find them, but must design and make your own telescope—from scratch. Or . . . moving right along here, how a half dozen college kids helped Vermont win a fifteen-year war against the outdoor-advertising industry to become the first state in the union to eliminate billboard blight. All this plus scintillating tours through 1) Vermont's oldest and only employee-owned flour company, 2) an interactive science museum, 3) a rescue haven for wounded birds of prey, and 4) the small Vermont hill town of Plymouth Notch, virtually unchanged from the days when President Coolidge ran his summer White House there, in the dance hall above his father's general store.

PHINEAS GAGE—HE NEEDED THIS JOB LIKE A HOLE IN THE HEAD

Cavendish

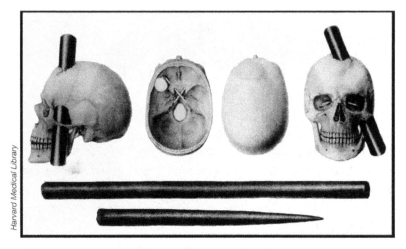

Imagine what poor Phineas thought when these x-rays came in. Oh, right. X-rays hadn't been invented yet. (These pictures are from a "prepared cranium.")

Bolted to a rock on Pleasant Street is a plaque commemorating "The Gage Accident." It was placed there in 1998, 150 years after a story that goes like this:

On September 13, 1848, Phineas P. Gage, a twenty-five-year-old Rutland & Burlington Railroad construction foreman, was setting dynamite charges to remove rock ledges impeding the railroad's expansion across Vermont. He first drilled a narrow hole in the rock and filled it halfway with blasting powder. Next came a fuse, and finally the powder was covered with protective sand and tamped down. Gage customarily signaled one of his men to pour in the sand before he tamped it down, with a rod designed for him by a local blacksmith. On this afternoon, however, he gestured for his partner to put in the sand and then was distracted by another worker. When he looked back and rammed his thirteen-pound tamping rod into the hole, he failed to see that his partner had not yet added the sand. His rod struck rock, created a spark, and whammo!

A tremendous blast propelled the 3-foot, 7-inch rod through Gage's left cheekbone, exiting the top of his skull at high speed, and landing, covered with blood and brains, more than 100 feet behind him. When his fellow workers reached the stunned Gage, they were amazed to see that he was not only alive but conscious. They carried him to an ox-drawn cart, which took him the three-quarters of a mile back to Cavendish. He was erect and got up the steps to the Adams Hotel with just a little assistance. According to neurobiologist Antonio Damasio in his book *Descartes' Error*, when the doctor arrived at Adams Hotel, Gage was seated on the front porch and greeted him by saying, "Doctor, here is business enough for you."

He was under the doctor's care for ten weeks and then discharged to his home in Lebanon, New Hampshire. Within two months he had completely recovered: He could walk, speak, and was pain free.

But it was soon clear that the Phineas Gage who went back to work was a completely different man. The hardworking, responsible, and popular Phineas was now, as his doctor wrote, ". . . fitful, irreverent, indulging in the grossest profanity . . . pertinaciously obstinate, yet capricious and vacillating. . . . [H]is mind was radically changed, so decidedly that his friends and acquaintances said he was 'no longer Gage.'"

Phineas was fired from his job in 1850 and spent about a year as a sideshow attraction at P. T. Barnum's New York museum, displaying his scars—and the tamping iron that caused them—to anyone willing to pay for the privilege. His health began to fail in 1859, and he moved to San Francisco to live with his mother. In 1860 he began to have epileptic seizures and died a few months later at the age of forty-two, buried with the rod that damaged him.

In 1990 an autopsy on Gage's exhumed body by Drs. Antonio and Hanna Damasio confirmed that the ruinous damage to the frontal lobes by the rod is what caused Gage's antisocial behavior, and that the seizures leading to his death were accident-related as well. Both his skull and the rod are part of a permanent exhibition at Harvard Medical School's Warren Anatomical Museum in Boston, Massachusetts.

In 1998, at the 150th commemoration of the tragic explosion, Phineas' rod was brought by armed guard from Harvard to

Cavendish for the ceremony. On September 13, its anniversary, walking tours to and from the respective sites are usually scheduled for commemoration.

Directions: To reach Cavendish, take exit 8 on I-91. Go west on Route 131 for 13 miles. The memorial plaque is in an empty lot at the corner of Route 131 and Pleasant Street. For more information and pictures, go to www.roadsideamerica.com/story/10858

YOUTUBE VIDEO:
"The Brain—Frontal Lobes and Behavior, the story of Phineas Gage" (13:42)
(Re-creation and analysis) 🍁

ALEKSANDR SOLZHENITSYN—RELUCTANT VERMONT RESIDENT

Cavendish

He was an artillery captain and fought the Nazis in World War II. But in 1945, after writing a letter criticizing Joseph Stalin, Aleksandr Solzhenitsyn was sentenced to eight years in prison and three more in enforced exile. In 1956 he settled in central Russia, where he taught mathematics and began to write.

In 1962 Solzhenitsyn submitted a short novel describing life in the forced labor camps of the Stalin era. *One Day in the Life of Ivan Denisovich* was an immediate sensation and inspired other writers to tell their own stories of imprisonment under Stalin's rule.

For the next twelve years Solzhenitsyn continued to write critically of the Stalin regime, to acclaim abroad and criticism at home. In 1970 he was awarded the Nobel Prize for Literature but dared not go to Stockholm to receive it for fear of being barred from returning to the Soviet Union. For his scorching indictment of prisons and labor camps (*The Gulag Archipelago*) in 1974, Solzhenitsyn was arrested for treason and exiled the following day.

But why choose Cavendish? Initially, Solzhenitsyn's first choice was Zurich, Switzerland. But people who found out where he lived continually asked him for favors, when all he wanted was peace and time to write. His second choice was the United States, and a lawyer suggested Cavendish, in the wooded and sparsely populated Green Mountain region of Vermont, not too different an atmosphere from his beloved Russia. He moved there in 1976.

"There is one more reason I came to live here," Solzhenitsyn told French journalist Bernard Pivot, one of the few to interview the writer while he lived in the United States. "It is the extraordinary wealth of American universities regarding Russian manuscripts, books, and documents pertaining to the 1917 revolution."

For the next eighteen years, Aleksandr Solzhenitsyn and his family lived in Cavendish. His wife, Natalia, served as his archivist, typist and advisor, and helped raise their three boys. The writer finished volumes two and three of *The Gulag Archipelago*, two other books of nonfiction, and four volumes of *The Red Wheel*, a history of the Russian revolution of 1917.

Solzhenitsyn and his wife then returned to Russia in 1994, where the author died in 2008. The boys, however, stayed to finish their education and became U.S. citizens. They still own the Vermont family home on Brook Road, in Cavendish. Ignat, a world-renowned pianist, is music director for the Chamber Orchestra of Philadelphia. He returned to his home state in 2007 to play an all-Brahms program in Brattleboro. His older brother Yermolay, who married a Russian girl, lives in Moscow and works at a U.S. firm. Younger brother Stephan is an environmental consultant in New York. "The interest in the Solzhenitzyns doesn't seem to die down," says Rich Svec, former town manager of Cavendish. "Just a few months ago, a Russian film crew was here preparing a documentary examining their lives in the U.S."

Directions: To reach Cavendish, take exit 8 on I-91. Go west on Route 131 for 13 miles.

YOUTUBE VIDEO:
"Aleksandr Solzhenitsyn: Writing The Red Wheel In Vermont" (1:58:18)
(A Brooks Memorial Library lecture by son Ignat in 2014. Long, but of interest to fans of this great novelist and Russian historian, Including photos and fascinating clips of family movies—bookmark it if you like, and come back when you have more time.) ❦

AMERICA'S OLDEST FLOUR COMPANY IS NOT SHOWING ITS AGE

Norwich

As soon as you hit the front door, you know that the folks at King Arthur Flour have things under control—in a nice way. On one wall is a video of a master baker giving instruction in the proper kneading of what will soon be a scrumptious loaf of bread. And he's right. Even with the sound off, I am aware that my technique needs help. I definitely could be more relaxed and allow the dough to stretch on its own, rather than pummel it into submission as is (soon to be "was") my practice. I definitely will be gentler with the limpa (Swedish rye bread) I bake next Christmas season. Ten feet from the TV monitor and under a glass-covered dome are free olive bread samples. Mmmm.

History first. The company was born in 1790 as the Sands, Taylor, and Wood Company, selling flour by the barrel off Long Wharf in Boston. It changed its name to King Arthur Flour after the owners saw a performance of King Arthur and the Knights of the Round Table. The extension of that metaphor within King Arthur Flour has since reached dizzying proportions, which need not concern us here.

All King Arthur flours have been free of bleach or chemicals of any kind for more than 200 years, which alone qualifies this company as a curiosity. Three of its eight flours are 100 percent organic. The company also sells a line of baking equipment, ingredients, mixes, and fresh-baked goods both in the store and through its *Baker's Catalogue*. (Freshly baked goods are shipped express.)

The press kit, courtesy of Allison Furbish, King Arthur's media coordinator the day I visited, tells us that the bakery produces up to 400 loaves of bread on a weekday, 600 on a weekend day, and that a team of eight bakers crank out the product in shifts of two. They start so early in the morning (3:00) that their lunch hour (actually only a half hour) is at 9:00. The pastry makers begin at 4:00 a.m., and each day bake dozens of different pastries for the Baker's Store and local inns and restaurants. (The daily bread-baking schedule customarily lists an average of six varieties.) On the day we visited, bread bakers Martin Philip and Becca Lambert were just finishing up batches of baguettes and Sonnenblumenbrot (or sunflower-seed bread). Martin bagged one of those five-syllable loaves just for me. Tasty!

In addition to straight baking, the company maintains a hotline staffed by eight seasoned bakers who answer 61,000 calls and e-mails a year from bakers with problems. Rebecca Faill, a cooking-school graduate and former caterer, has heard it all, from a woman trying to duplicate her neighbor's award-winning pie to a monk fine-tuning a bread recipe for his monastery.

Directions: King Arthur's Flour is a gray building with red trim located on U.S. Route 5, 1/2 mile south of I-91 exit 13, on the left just past the car dealership. The Baker's Store is located at 135 Route 5 South, Norwich, Vermont. Store hours are Monday–Sunday, 7:30 a.m.–6:00 p.m. Closed New Year's Day, Easter Sunday, Independence Day, Thanksgiving Day, and Christmas Day. Read more about King Arthur Flour and its many services on www.kingarthurflour.com or call (802) 649-3361.

YOUTUBE VIDEOS:
"King Arthur Flour Channel" (A series of dozens of videos of varying lengths that will keep you busy for hours— or minutes—depending on your level of Interest in the baking process.) ❦

SCIENCE A KID CAN GROOVE ON

Norwich

Waiting at the front desk for a curatorial assistant to tell me about the Montshire Museum of Science, I saw a six-year-old dart from behind an exhibit 20 feet away to retrieve a yellow ping-pong ball from the carpeted floor. Then another. And another. I walked closer to see what the breakdown might be. Then I saw the boy's father, on his knees, putting those balls into a "Tube Tunnel" that demonstrated one of a number of air-pressure-related physics principles. It was then that I first appreciated the museum's laid-back, interactive genius.

**The Montshire's mission is to create and nurture curiosity
about the physical and natural world.**

More than sixty hands-on exhibits relating to the natural sciences, astronomy, ecology, and technology can be found both inside and out on the museum's 110-acre site. In addition to the permanent exhibits, revolving exhibits are maintained for several months at a time to highlight current developments in science or provide a local venue for exhibits traveling among several major cities. "Toys: The Inside Story," for example, revealed how pulleys, circuits, gears, cams, and other mechanisms make familiar toys, such as an Etch-a-Sketch or a jack-in-the-box, work.

A network of nature trails includes a number of additional exhibits, the Human Sundial, and the Planet Walk, which requires a 1.6-mile hike to reach Pluto.

The Montshire is designed to appeal to all ages, much like an animated movie produced to attract both adults and children. Most indoor exhibit spaces and all restrooms are wheelchair accessible, as are the walking trails.

Directions: The Montshire is located off I-91, exit 13, 5 miles north of White River Junction, directly across the Connecticut River from Dartmouth College in New Hampshire, at 1 Monstshire Road. The museum is open daily, 10:00 a.m. to 5:00 p.m. For more information go to www.montshire.org, or call (802) 649-2200.

YouTube Videos:
"Leafcutter Ant Colony at Montshire Museum, VT" (:51)
"Montshire Museum Turtles" (1:15)
(two to begin with; many more available) 🍁

THE PRESIDENT COOLIDGE SUMMER HOME— JUST ABOVE HIS STORE

Plymouth Notch

Back in President Coolidge's day there were no grand presidential libraries. His papers, and those of his predecessors, are in the Library of Congress. But let's say there were—grand presidential libraries, that is. Chances are that rather than raise millions of dollars for a monument to himself, our thirtieth president more likely would have refurbished the Wilder Barn on his property and replaced the agricultural equipment exhibition that now occupies it with appropriate records of his years in the White House.

Bill Jenney, regional historic site administrator at the birthplace and boyhood home of Calvin Coolidge, recounts the night that the presidential guard was changed: "In August of 1923, when Vice President Coolidge happened to be up here visiting his family, word came that President Warren Harding had died. [Coolidge] had to be sworn in immediately, and the only available official was his father, who was also the local notary public. Actually, there was a second ceremony with a federal judge back in Washington, because there was some debate as to whether a state official could swear in a federal officer. That Coolidge was sworn in by his father in the family homestead, in the middle of the night, by the light of a kerosene lamp, played quite well in the presidential campaign for the 1924 election, when he ran in his own right, and which he won with the highest plurality then known."

John Calvin Coolidge Jr. was born on July 4, 1872, within yards of the room in which his father swore him in as president 51 years later. He graduated from Amherst College with honors and entered law and politics in Northampton, Massachusetts. Some think that because Coolidge was an accidental president, he had little taste for the top office. But slowly and methodically, he went up the Republican political ladder, from councilman in Northampton to governor of Massachusetts. His forceful intervention in the Boston police strike of 1919 propelled him to national attention, and President Warren G. Harding named him as his running mate in the 1920 election. Twenty-nine months later, Harding died of a heart attack at fifty-seven.

The small Vermont hill town of Plymouth Notch is virtually unchanged from the days during which President Coolidge ran his summer White House here in the dance hall above his father's general store. His entire staff consisted of a secretary and a stenographer. The last summer before his reelection, however, this threesome was augmented by a Secret Service detail of eighteen, because of death threats Coolidge had received. That summer he also was recovering from the death of his son, also Calvin Jr., whose infected blister from playing tennis at the White House courts with his brother John led to blood poisoning. Coolidge declined to run for a second term on his own, believing that his one year in office after Harding's death should count as a full term.

The homes of Coolidge's family and neighbors on the site are carefully preserved, as are the village church, general store, and cheese factory—still making cheese using the original 1890 recipe. Also on-site are a visitors' center, two museum stores, two walking trails, a restaurant, and a picnic area. To visit the steep, hillside cemetery where Calvin Coolidge rests with seven generations of his family, turn right out of the visitors' parking area onto Route 100A, and turn left onto Lynds Hill Road, about 100 yards south.

Directions: The President Calvin Coolidge State Historic Site is located 6 miles south of U.S. Route 4 on State Route 100A. The site is open from the last weekend in May until mid-October, daily 9:30 a.m. to 5:00 p.m. For more specific information and to see a list of events, go to www.historicvermont.org/coolidge or call (802) 672-3773.

YOUTUBE VIDEOS:
"President Calvin Coolidge State Historic Site Vermont Fall" (1:38) (Brief look at the site's exterior—most others available, like this one, are home videos with limited production values.) ❧

QUECHEE GORGE, VERMONT'S "LITTLE GRAND CANYON"

Quechee

As a matter of scale, if Quechee Gorge and the Grand Canyon are being used in the same sentence, *minuscule* is probably more accurate a word than *little*. Still, as a part of 600-acre Quechee Gorge State Park, it is still the most spectacular river gorge in Vermont. Just east of Quechee Village, the Ottauquechee River turns south and plunges into the narrow, rocky cleft of Quechee Gorge—165 feet deep and more than a mile long. Quechee Gorge is what remains of a waterfall that carved its way north over thousands of years, eroding tough metamorphic rock until the formidable barrier was cut clean through.

Enter the path along the gorge just north of the east side of the U.S. Route 4 bridge. To the right is a picnic area, and a quarter mile farther is the old Dewey Wool Mill, no longer in operation, and the waterfall that made it work. Walking back under the bridge will take you to the gorge outlook—but be careful. This walk is more strenuous than the one to Dewey Wool Mill.

About 1,500 feet before the bridge (on the left going toward Woodstock) is Quechee Gorge State Park Campground.

**At right can be seen the result of erosion so massive
it moved the Outtauquechee River waterfall far
enough north to create Quechee Gorge**

Directions: Quechee Gorge can be reached by taking exit 1 on Interstate 89 toward Woodstock, and then going 7 miles southeast on U.S. Route 4. Admission is free. An annual highlight is the Quechee Gorge Hot Air Balloon Festival on Father's Day weekend. Thousands attend, so if you're interested, make reservations early. For more information visit the park's Web site at www.vtstateparks. com/htm/quechee.cfm.

YouTube Video
"Quechee Gorge" Christopher Schmidt (3:37)
The quadcopter (drone) perspectives you see here won't be available on foot. ❧

VERMONT HOME FOR WOUNDED BIRDS OF PREY

Quechee

Environmental educator Hannah Putnam describes the habitat and habits of a Harris Hawk to a VINS audience. Hannah's work with program birds embraces a number of birds and audience levels.

There's a lot more to the Vermont Institute of Natural Science (VINS) than its rescue program for raptors and songbirds, but that seems its best-known activity. Each year more than 400 hawks and hummingbirds, geese and grackles, waxwings and warblers are welcomed to the nature center and rehabilitated. Some are highway hit-and-run victims; others have collided with a window; still others arrive orphaned, with no visible means of support. A number of other rehabilitation specialists with ties to VINS throughout the state and in New Hampshire are on call for the rescue and rehab of hundreds more, as well as a like number of mammals.

"We ask questions to find out what the injury might be, and whether the bird actually needs assistance or not," says Stephanie Hanwell, lead wildlife keeper and one of the specialists on call. "In the summer, for example, we get lots of baby-bird calls. When they're fledglings, they're just out hopping on their own, even though their parents are still taking care of them. But because they're not able to fly more than a foot or two, sometimes people think they're injured." A lot of deductive questioning determines the next step: whether to refer the caller to a local rehabilitator or, if the caller is reporting an injured mammal (the Quechee center takes in only birds), to refer them to the appropriate rehabber, or to one of the ten or so veterinarians throughout the state who work with VINS.

About 50 percent of the birds treated can be released in the wild again. Some die, of course, and the rest—primarily raptors—are either put up for adoption or kept as "program" or "exhibit" birds. The oldest resident is a twenty-five-year-old turkey vulture, trained as a program bird to maintain its dignity and composure perched on the heavily gloved lower arm of a staffer or volunteer. The handler, in turn, has been trained to describe to visitors the reason the bird is at the center and its place in the wild when it lived there, and then answer any questions visitors may have. Exhibit birds, largely untrainable for various reasons—and also injured or otherwise unable to return to their natural habitats—are kept in large enclosed settings designed to approximate their environment in the wild as closely as practicable. When possible, they are hooked up with roommates of their own species.

Education is a strong VINS component, as evident in VINS marketing director Molly Hutchins's description of the curriculum on our tour of the center. "We put on a week-by-week day nature camp here in Quechee; at our Manchester, Vermont, site; and in Hanover, New Hampshire. Five hundred and twenty-five kids went through our camp program this summer, quadruple what it was last year." Twice a day, educators conduct half-hour programs that tell kids about whatever program bird is assisting in that particular demonstration. "The other two times a day," says Molly, "kids are taken on one of a number of nature hikes over the 3 miles of trails we have here in Quechee. There are four completely different programs every day."

Other regularly scheduled programs for groups of ten or more focus on nature walks and demonstrations of a wide variety of topics, from exploring natural habitats of Vermont to learning about the intricacies of bird flight. All are designed to enhance environmental learning and citizenship. Look for details about this, as well as an intriguing Citizen Science program involving more than 1,000 volunteer citizen scientists, on the comprehensive VINS Web site, listed below.

VINS's outreach program for the schools similarly includes natural history and environmental science. "The introduction to these topics to preschoolers in camp sessions is presented more comprehensively in the programs available to schools, either in workshops at the center, or by educators who go into the schools of Vermont and New Hampshire." Molly Hutchins continues, "In addition, we have just started a program offering teacher development workshops, where we teach teachers to teach the natural sciences. This assistance is offered pre-K through the twelfth grade."

Directions: The VINS Nature Center is located 1/4 mile west of the Quechee Gorge on the right-hand side of U.S. Route 4. From I-89, take exit 1 to U.S. Route 4 West. VINS is open to the public from May 1 through October 31, 10:00 a.m.–5:00 p.m., seven days a week; and from November 1 through April 30, 10:00 a.m.–4:00 p.m., Wednesday–Sunday. Admission is $9 for adults, $8 for seniors, and $7 for youth three to eighteen, with children two and under free. For more information visit www.vinsweb.org or call (802) 359-5000.

YouTube Video:
"Hand-feeding a Sharp-shinned Hawk" (4:08)
(Nice Introduction to the work of these specialists. Several others available.) ❦

THE SKY CLOSE-UP

Springfield

The Springfield Telescope Company

**The telescope exhibition at a Stellafane Amateur
Astronomers' Convention**

Stellafane, the home of the Springfield Telescope Makers, Inc., is located on 85 acres of Breezy Hill, just outside of Springfield. Its name is Latin for "shrine to the stars." An ancient metaphor, "Standing on the shoulders of giants," typifies an awareness by Stellafane club members that their accomplishments have been largely inspired by Russell W. Porter, the club's founder in 1923, and the Giant of this story.

Porter was born in Springfield in 1871, graduated from Vermont Academy in 1889, and studied engineering and architecture at the University of Vermont and Massachusetts Institute of Technology. A longtime interest in the Arctic then led him on several trips to Greenland and points north. On a 1903 expedition he was stranded for an astonishing three years when his ship was crushed by ice and sank in the Russian Arctic.

Ann Thompson brings her fifth-grade class to Stellafane every year to learn the latest about astronomical developments—a week or so after Ken Slater visits the class in Cavendish to help them tie astronomy to everyday life.

Porter finally settled in Port Clyde, Maine, where over a six-year period he started an artists' colony, built cottages for a motel enterprise, tried farming, and married the local postmistress. It was then that his good friend James Hartness introduced him to astronomy. This led to an interest in telescope-making, and ultimately to a move back to Springfield with his wife and daughter to work for Hartness at his machine company. With his boss's encouragement, Porter started a telescope- making class. After mastering this craft, fifteen of the class members created Springfield Telescope Makers, and as a basic condition of membership required that those interested both design and build a telescope to the group's exacting specifications. Porter designed a unique turret telescope near the Stellafane clubhouse, completed in 1931.

Russell Porter became so good at his fifth—or maybe sixth— occupation that he was recruited in 1927 to work on the design of the Mt. Palomar telescope, soon to be the world's largest. His legacy lasts, with his name given to the moon's Crater Porter, as well as to Crater Porter on Mars.

Stellafane Vice-President Ken Slater counts among his early heroes not only Russell Porter but astronomer and educator Carl Sagan, from whom he took an astronomy course at Cornell University in the 1970s. (He'll tell you an excellent Sagan anecdote if you ask him.) In 2008, after retiring from a successful electrical engineering career, Ken and his family moved to Chester, not coincidentally just eight miles from Springfield's Stellafane, which he had joined in 1997. His computer expertise led him to become the club's webmaster, and eventually a vice president. He is now working on his sixth telescope.

One of Ken's interests is lifelong learning, which has led to an annual exchange with an aware public-school teacher interested in passing on to her pupils some of the principles of astronomy.

As Ken recalls it, "Ann Thompson, who teaches fifth grade at Cavendish Elementary School [also state winner of the 2011 Presidential Science Teaching Award], emailed the club several years ago, writing that she was doing a module on astronomy for her science class. She asked if someone could tell her class a little bit about astronomy—and specifically, what went on at Stellafane.

"So every year I go up there and teach a class, including how astronomy relates to everyday life—lunar cycles, tides, and the like, for example—and then the next week or so the class come here and we'll do a few exercises about sundials, examine artifacts in the clubhouse, and discuss whatever the current astronomical topic happens to be."

Stellafane also gives telescopes to schools, based on their donations each year. "We're happy to do this," says Ken. "In the 1920s and earlier, telescopes cost a fortune—as much as $20,000 in today's money. They're a lot less today—$200 or so can buy a fine telescope—but many schools can't afford even those modest prices. So we're happy to do what we can to increase interest in astronomy."

http://stellafane.org. The site not only thoroughly describes the club's past and present, but provides enough additional information to be a primer for the science of astronomy.

YouTube Videos:
0400 Stellafane Springfield 2014 (2:02)
(Watch for narrator Ken Slater checking out the red telescope at 1:30)

Stellafane Amateur Astronomers Convention 2017 🍁

HEADQUARTERS FOR MEN (VALARI FREEBORNE, PROP.)

Springfield

photo courtesy of the author

Valari doing what she does best—the conversation is as good as the trim.

It's been a while since barbershops discriminated—at least by gender. And despite the title, this one doesn't either. "Headquarters for Men" just happened to be the name of the shop Valari Freeborne wanted to buy fifteen years ago, and under the terms of sale, the name came with the shop. You can tell males are among her favorite customers, though, by a prominently positioned sentiment: "Men: They're like tires; it never hurts to have a spare."

Laura, Minerva, Lolita, and Tracy, though, the four well-dressed mannequins in the window, send a somewhat different message to someone entering the shop for the first time—subtly and simultaneously welcoming distaff clientele. Meanwhile, in the shop proper, more racily clad models (one in chain mail and outfitted by Val), appeal to some of the "spare tires" who happen by.

The graffiti on three of the four walls give some indication of the owner's far-flung leanings and set the tone for random conversations. "Hey you! Turn off your cellphone. Thank you"; "Sarcasm—one of the free services we offer"; "Complaint Department: Ring bell for service" is actually a non-working mousetrap. A weekly changing Employee Handbook to "All Stylists" (though she works alone) lists ever-more-draconian workday restrictions: Val's six-shelf book collection for all to read includes titles such as *Dealing with Difficult People; Duh! A Stupid History of the Stupid Human Race;* and a 1901 novel called *Quincy Adams Sawyer: A Story of New England Home Life*, by Charles Felton Pidgin.

Throughout the day, Val maintains a non-stop-give-and-take with six to eight customers at any given time, about half of whom are waiting for haircuts. The rest either already have been shorn, or just dropped in to listen to whatever political, social, or nonsensical topic happens to come up. On a morning I came in, followed ten minutes later by a state police officer in need of a trim, Val welcomed a pharmacy employee delivering her a prescription.

"Ah, here comes my drug dealer," said Val. The young man said nothing but seemed a bit edgy. When he stopped to give her a receipt, she added, "Doesn't that make you a dealer?"

"No," he said, glancing quickly at the lawman, "just nervous." The officer, a regular and no stranger to Val's schtick, hadn't looked up from his newspaper during the entire exchange.

At the back end of the 20 x 30-foot Headquarters are two dozen or so "black velvet" paintings—called by some the pinnacle of tackiness; by others, classic works of art. Most have been contributed by customers and friends for an annual Christmas sale. Val "marks down" various works from, say, $400 to $10, with proceeds going to the Springfield Humane Society.

The shop has donated between $200 and $400 annually since 2009, but this year a house fire in Chester killed the family pets. When two local pre-teens came in selling baked goods to raise money for the family just before Christmas, Val decided—with Humane Society endorsement—that this year's donation should go to the Chester family.

Yeah, she's tough and sardonic, but don't bet against her in any competition for Den Mother of the Year in a Connecticut River Valley-wide election. You'd lose.

Walk-ins only, 9-5 Tuesday through Friday, 7:30-12 Saturday. 802.885.9595 ❦

HOW THE SIMPSONS CHOSE VERMONT AS HOME

Springfield

Here was the competition: Oregon, Illinois, Massachusetts, Colorado, Nebraska, Missouri, Louisiana, Florida, New Jersey, Michigan, Ohio, Kentucky, and Tennessee. Illinois was a close second; Florida was last. Vermont got the job done. At stake was the coronation of one of these 14 states' Springfield as the *real* home of the Simpsons.

What made the difference? Each entrant submitted a three- to five-minute film, showcasing its community's "Simpsons Spirit." Twentieth Century–Fox provided interested parties with key film-making tools, including a digital video camera, *The Simpsons Movie* posters, and enough "Simpson-yellow" paint to last Homer through several nuclear meltdowns.

We'll let you judge each entry for yourself, but first we need to talk about the woeful disadvantage that Springfield, Vermont had to overcome. Why would the ultimate winner not even have been *invited* to compete originally? That's right. Our Springfield people found out at the eleventh hour and weren't even able to start production on their video until two weeks before the deadline. (Yes, we are outraged, one more time.)

Well, whoever the perpetrators were, it didn't work! Yeah, baby, we came sailin' through. Final score: Vermont 1; Tennessee, Ohio, Oregon, and everybody else 0. In a futile attempt to prove that Hollywood has a heart, each of the other thirteen Springfields had a screening of their own, the night before *The Simpsons Movie* hit theaters nationwide late in July of 2007. And lest you think otherwise, this big-screen premiere was the real reason for all this folderol in the first place. To see the thirteen competing Springfield videos, go to: www.usatoday.com/life/movies/simpsons-contest.htm.

Directions: Just about anyone in Springfield will be happy to answer your Simpson questions, or anything else about the town. Just ask. Take I-91 exit 7 west into town on Route 11.

YOUTUBE VIDEOS:
"The Simpsons, Springfield, Windsor County, Vermont, United States, North America" (1:51).

(And many others) ❦

VERMONT'S FIFTEEN-YEAR WAR AGAINST BILLBOARDS

Weston

To learn how Vermont became the first state in the nation to ban billboards, a good place to start is the Orton family dining room table, back in the 1950s. Vrest Orton, a writer, activist, and founder of the Vermont Country Store chain (two stores), was passionate about the quality of his state's future, and frequently shared these opinions with his family.

"Yes, my father was one of the early supporters of getting rid of billboards in Vermont," says Lyman Orton, Vrest's son. In supporting this position over the years, Vrest Orton did not endear himself to the powerful outdoor advertising industry, who predicted that eliminating billboards would be the end of business as they knew it. "About the same thing they said when we made bottles and cans returnable," says Lyman.

**Thanks to Vermont legislator Ted Riehle and Vermont Country Store
founder Vrest Orton, beautiful roadside scenes like this have been
available throughout the state since billboards were banned In 1967.**

Orton went off to Middlebury College in the fall of 1959 with
a strong recollection of those hours spent at the dinner table. At
the same time, a phenomenon arrived to crystalize the pro- and
anti-billboard debate.

"Have you heard of Seashell City?" Lyman asks. I hadn't.
"Seashell City was a couple of nondescript buildings painted bright
red on Route 7 between Brandon and Leicester—ten or fifteen
miles south of Middlebury. They sold seashells . . . in the middle
of Vermont! A few months after the buildings appeared, about fifty
billboards went up—seemingly all the way from Massachusetts to
Canada—on both sides of the road and painted bright red with
white letters. They were just huge and went up so quickly they
seemed to have grown out of the ground. When you went in the
buildings, there were just these baskets full of seashells and other
little knickknacks. Underwhelming, at best."

Seashell City helped provide a focus for the outrage on billboards, though, and what could happen all over the state unless
something was done about it. As a college student who had lis-
tened well to his father and shared his taste for activism, Lyman
acted.

"I rounded up a few fraternity brothers, and we went out late at night and began cutting the billboards down. We started with axes, but the support timbers were almost as big as telephone poles, so we knew that wouldn't work. We bought crosscut saws, and over a couple of years we got rid of quite a few of them. It made the papers, of course, but we never got caught. I guess the statute of limitations is up, so it's safe to tell this story!"

Enter Ted Riehle, a Vermont legislator who took on the outdoor advertising lobby and a few of its business allies head-on. "He was the legislative hero for this issue," says Lyman. "I remember him visiting my father at our store a couple of times." In 1967, Riehle introduced legislation to ban all billboards except for small signs advertising local businesses and agricultural products—as well as to tear down all existing billboards. With the support of garden clubs throughout the state and other anti-billboard merchants, Governor Phil Hoff signed the bill into law in 1968. In 1974, Vermont felled its last billboard.

These days, Lyman limits his anti-billboard activism to board membership of Scenic America, which he calls "a small band of brothers and sisters born out of the Lady Bird Johnson–inspired Highway Beautification Act." Since then, says Orton, "that act has been amended so many times it could be called 'The Highway Desecration Act.'" Scenic America is the watchdog against the billboard industry, whose goal is to overturn or weaken anti-billboard legislation at federal, state, and local levels. So far so good. Forty years and counting.

To learn more about the Orton family and their activities, visit: www.orton.org; www.scenicamerica.org; and www.vermontcountrystore.com.

YOUTUBE VIDEO
Fall Foliage in Stowe, Vermont—Don't Miss It! (1:33) 🍁

MOUNT ASCUTNEY—NEW ENGLAND'S PREMIER HANG GLIDING MOUNTAIN

Windsor

courtesy of the author

**In times of need, some step forward. On this day the author was
selected as crew chief when no one volunteered. To the surprise of
all present, the pilot launched without mishap.**

Ever wonder what it would feel like to launch yourself off the top
of a 3,150-foot mountain (more than twice as high as Chicago's
mammoth Sears Tower)? You could ask one of the ten to thirty
hang gliding pilots who take off from either the South or West Peak
launching site on Mount Ascutney every reasonably nice day. Or
you could take a tandem flight with a licensed pilot. All depends
on your level of interest.

If you just want to watch, you can either drive up or hike. The
drive is a wandering path of switchbacks beginning at the entrance
to Mount Ascutney State Park, and through the forest to the upper
parking lot, at 2,800 feet. (A network of hiking trails will take you
directly to the summit, another 350 feet above.) The trails to both
launching sites are well marked.

Take the trail at the far northwest side of the parking lot and go left at the first fork. (The right fork goes to the lookout tower at the top of the mountain.) Continue until you come to a clearing, which is the West Peak launching site. On all but the calmest days, a wire crew of two (one on each wing) or three (another at the nose in rougher weather) is needed to assist with the launches.

Early or late in the day, when not enough experienced pilots are waiting to handle wire-crew duties, bystanders are asked to help out. Listen carefully to instructions if you volunteer for the wire crew, because the pilot's life could be in your hands. (A trusting lot, those hang glider pilots—in addition to being plucky.)

Tom Lanning is one of very few hang-gliding pilots to make it nonstop from Mt. Ascutney to the New Hampshire shore, 93 miles away. Here is an excerpt from his account of the four-hour trip, printed in the Vermont Hang Gliding Association newsletter:

"Although we battled black flies, soggy ground, and a brisk crosswind on launch, we were soon airborne and soaring nicely in a WNW wind I measured at 25 mph. . . . As I topped out over 6,000 feet, I could finally see I-89, Concord, and Manchester [New Hampshire]. I decided to work across a cloud-bridge and was rewarded with an easy 14-mile ride.

"Finally I saw the coast in the distance and started working on a plan to land on the beach. As I crossed Hampton Beach I gained a couple of hundred feet. I flew to the water's edge and down the coastline. As I flew back up the beach people were waving and shouting at me, and I waved back. I returned to the south end, did a number of slow "S" turns and floated onto the shore with a no-step landing.

"A crowd soon formed around me, and I answered the usual array of questions. After calling home, I broke down my glider, and was surprised at how quickly my friends Dan and Greg arrived to pick me up. After high-fives we loaded up and headed to a restaurant for clams, lobster, and steamers on an outside deck and watched the sun set. What a great ending to a great day."

Camping, hiking, and cross-country skiing are also among the attractions at Mount Ascutney, which is one of Vermont's very few monadnocks, in this instance meaning not part of the Green Mountains.

Directions: From Interstate 91 (exit 8), go .2 miles east on Route 131 to the stoplight; turn left on U.S. Route 5, traveling for 1.2 miles, and then bear left on Route 44A for 1 mile. Fans of *Death Wish* 1–5 may pay their respects to Charles Bronson at his grave site in the Brownsville Cemetery at the foot of Mount Ascutney. For more information go to www.vtstateparks.com/htm/ascutney.cfm.

YouTube Video:
"Hang Gliding Mt. Ascutney, VT" (6:01).
(Good feel for the amount of control a pilot has. The camera shuts off just before what Tom Lansing definitely would not call a "no-step" landing.) ❦

WORLD'S LONGEST TWO-SPAN COVERED BRIDGE

Windsor

Every bridge between Vermont and New Hampshire on the Connecticut River is owned by the State of New Hampshire. Who said life was fair?

As you may recall in Chapter 2 (relax, we've discarded the pop quiz), back in 1764 King George III whimsically handed over most of Vermont to both New Hampshire and New York. (This is one reason Vermont seceded from the colonies in the first place.) New Hampshire wound up with the Connecticut River, all the way to the low-water mark on the west bank. For some reason Vermont and New Hampshire couldn't agree that the boundary should be in the middle of the river, as other states have when haggling about river ownership. New Hampshire stubbornly insisted on the whole megillah.

Those decisions in the 1700s were made before dams were built on the river. Today, the boundary between Vermont and New Hampshire actually extends as much as a third of the way across the river, because the dams have flooded the valleys. This has been a sore point for many Vermonters ever since, particularly after a Supreme Court decision in 1934 validated King George's 170-year-old decision.

The Windsor-Cornish Bridge—or as New Hampshirites obviously would have it, the Cornish-Windsor Bridge—is, at 449.4 feet, the longest wooden bridge in the country and the longest two-span wooden bridge in the world. Ed Varna, in *Covered Bridges of Vermont*, delivers his own double zinger in the direction of his cross-river neighbors: "This must be a treacherous location, since there were three previous bridges at this crossing of the Connecticut River, all destroyed by floods. . . . The bridge underwent major restoration work during the late 1980s, with neighboring New Hampshire footing most of the $4.65 million bill."

Ouch. And ouch.

You have to wonder, though: If Vermonters can put in and take out river craft on either bank, if Vermont fishing licenses include all of the Connecticut River and not just the sliver apportioned to us, and if New Hampshire pays for bi-state bridge repair, Vermont really doesn't have such a bad deal. That is, they didn't until Vilas Bridgegate.

That fracas is detailed in Chapter 2. Briefly, it has to do with the Vilas Bridge being closed for repairs in 2009, and New Hampshire's refusal to pay a nickel to repair it. That was the deal that state insisted on, so why it remains a deadlock is a matter of dispute.

(Rumors persist that the Windsor Bridge has been overtaken by another in terms of record length, but not convincingly. Prove otherwise and we'll step down without a whimper. (Wikipedia's "Cornish-Windsor Covered Bridge" entry tells the whole story). See Chapter 2 for details.

Directions: To reach the Windsor-Cornish Bridge, take I-91 exit 8 (from the south) or exit 9 (from the north). From Main Street (U.S. Route 5) at the south end of Windsor Village, turn onto Bridge Street just south of the stoplight. For more information and pictures, visit www.coveredbridgesite.com/nh/cornish_windsor.html.

YOUTUBE VIDEO:
"949 Productions: Cornish-Windsor Covered Bridge (1:05)
(Interesting drone-driven trip over and around the bridge) ❧

BIRTH OF THE VERMONT NATION

Windsor

public domain

**In Windsor in 1777, delegates of the new Republic of Vermont
drafted a constitution even more progressive than the U.S.
Constitution signed ten years later in Philadelphia.**

The first constitution of the "Free and Independent State of Vermont"
was adopted on July 8, 1777, less than a year after the signing of the
Declaration of Independence, at Elijah West's Tavern, in Windsor.
The present state of Vermont was occupied by New Hampshire,
New York, and Massachusetts for much of the eighteenth century.
These were not benevolent neighbors. Vermont residents fumed at
the large fees New York laid on them just for transferring title to
their lands, for example.

For this and other reasons, they decided to form their own republic and wrote a constitution modeled after Benjamin Franklin's for the State of Pennsylvania. The Vermont framers went further, however. Their constitution was the first to prohibit slavery, and the first to grant voting rights without regard to property ownership or specific income.

At about the time the Constitution was being finalized, British forces attacked and captured the fort complex of Ticonderoga, just across Lake Champlain. The British pursued the retreating American forces and met General Arthur St. Clair's rearguard at Hubbardton on July 7. Even though 1,000 Americans, including Ethan Allen and a band of 200 Green Mountain Men, successfully delayed the British advance, many residents on the west side of the Green Mountains had to run for their lives. Word of these alarming events reached Windsor on July 8, and the constitution was voted on—accompanied by a violent thunderstorm—just before the convention disbanded.

Vermont's Old Constitution House is a restoration of Elijah West's Tavern, which was located nearby. The land for the new location was donated by the family of William Evarts, who served as secretary of state for President Rutherford B. Hayes and was chief counsel for the defense in the impeachment trial of President Andrew Johnson.

Directions: It is located at 16 Main Street at the northern end of the village of Windsor on U.S. Route 5, accessible from exits 8 and 9 on I-91. The museum is open to the public 11:00 a.m. to 5:00 p.m. on Saturday and Sunday from late May through mid-October. For more information call (802) 672-3773 or visit www.historicvermont.org/constitution. ❧

FIRST SKI TOW IN AMERICA

In January 1934, the first ski tow in the United States was set up on Clinton Gilbert's farm in Woodstock. This simple rope tow, powered by a Model T Ford engine, helped begin Vermont's far-reaching ski industry and gave the sport a much-needed lift.

"When the rope tow started at Woodstock," says Charlie Asenowich, Vermont's self-styled first and most durable ski bum, "we teenagers at school got excited about skiing. Shortly thereafter, ski areas began cropping up like mushrooms."

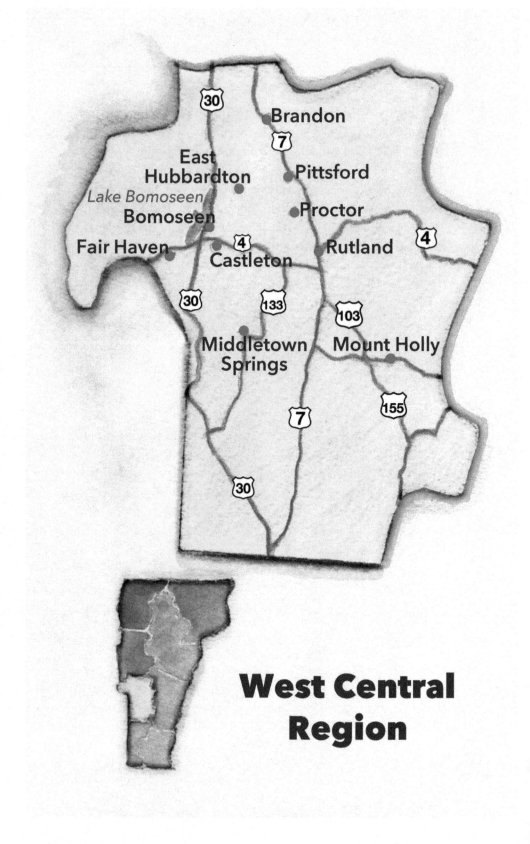

30

Brandon

7

East
Hubbardton

Lake Bomoseen

Bomoseen

Pittsford

Proctor

4

Fair Haven

4

Castleton

Rutland

30

133

103

Middletown
Springs

Mount Holly

7

155

30

West Central
Region

5

WEST CENTRAL

Those of you old enough to remember Harpo Marx and Alexander Woolcott knew they had roots in Vermont, didn't you? That may be overstating their ties to this state a bit, but they and several friends did spend from two weeks to an entire summer in the 1930s and early 40s at Woolcott's cabin on Neshobe Island. We offer here a glimpse of the Neshobe Island Club and what remained of the legendary Algonquin Round Table.

In Proctor is a thirty-two-room, thirteen-fireplace, brick castle in the Flemish style, on the outside. But inside you'll discover a mixture of Queen Anne, Scottish baronial, Dutch neo-renaissance, and Romanesque revival styles. (Head spinning yet?) This is the Wilson Castle, named for the owner. The builder sold it at auction after the death of his wife, whose millions provided the original financing. Mrs. Johnson (the wife), for her investment, insisted that all the bricks be imported from England. It was her money, after all. And she was English, after all. Docent coordinator Sheila Kelley will cheerfully discuss the castle's spirit presence to the extent of your interest.

LAKE BOMOSEEN, A HARPO MARX HIDEAWAY

Bomoseen

Neshobe Island, in the middle of Lake Bomoseen, was named in honor of an Abenaki Indian scout who helped Ethan Allen and his Green Mountain Boys find and defeat the New Yorkers at

credit: Ralph F. Stitt [Public domain] via Wikimedia Commons

Arthur "Harpo" Marx, 1931. When he wasn't enjoying summers at the lake, Harpo was making hilarious movies with brothers Groucho and Chico.

Fort Ticonderoga in 1775. As late as the early twentieth century, Abenaki Indians returned to Indian Point every summer, to camp near the island.

From the mid-1920s until the early 1940s, Neshobe Island was the summer and weekend home of writer and critic Alexander Woollcott. It was also the retreat of a number of his celebrity friends, including Dorothy Parker, Helen Hayes, Ethel Barrymore, Irving Berlin, and Teddy Roosevelt Jr., who landed his seaplane on the lake when he came up to Neshobe from New York.

Woollcott's good friend Harpo Marx spent many weekends there, describing its eight acres as having a "wonderful variety of terrain and vegetation: miniature meadows, hills, and cliffs; quarries and beaches; wildflowers, flowering vines and bushes; [and] maples and evergreens," all just a quarter mile from the mainland. Woollcott built a rambling stone house on a ridge overlooking the lake on all sides, which became his permanent home the last seven years of his life.

As Harpo writes in his autobiography, *Harpo Speaks*, "the natives, in true Vermont fashion, didn't bother anybody who didn't bother them, but the tourists were a nosy bunch. . . . One day novelist Alice Duer Miller went for a walk and rushed back to report that a group of tourists had rowed over from the mainland and were having a [somewhat raucous] picnic on the beach.

"I volunteered to deal with the interlopers. I stripped off all my clothes, put on my red wig, smeared myself with mud, and went whooping and war dancing down to the shore, brandishing an axe. The tourists snatched up their things, threw them into the boat, and rowed away fast enough to have won a . . . regatta. That put an end to the snooping that season."

Directions: To reach Lake Bomoseen, take U.S. Route 4 west to exit 4, in Castleton. Turn right on Route 30 and then go 2 miles to Bomoseen. To get more information on the state park at Lake Bomoseen, visit www.vtstateparks.com/htm/bomoseen.cfm or call (802) 265-4242.

YOUTUBE VIDEOS
"Neshobe Island" (9:03)(
Long on talk, but outstanding for tour of grounds and Neshobe Island Club resurrection)

"Chico and Harpo Marx piano duet" (2:49)
(With their customary hilarity) ❧

QUEEN CONNIE—REBAR AND CONCRETE
(16 TONS, 20 FEET TALL)

"A larger-than-life gorilla lofts a Volkswagen Beetle as though it were an Olympic torch." *Car and Driver* (January 1991)

Sculptor—T. J. Neill, 1984

Location: Pioneer Auto Sales, 2829 U.S. Route 7, Brandon, Vermont

First Prize: "Carchitectural Wonders," Car and Driver, January 1991

Runner-up: "Four Giant-Sized Human Legs Support a Compact Sedan" (Prague, Czechoslovakia)

Second runner-up: "A Yugo Plunges through the Roof of a Barn" (Littleton, Colorado)

THE PIVOTAL BATTLE OF HUBBARDTON

East Hubbardton

Here's what led up to the Battle of Hubbardton: In 1775 General Benedict Arnold, Ethan Allen, and eighty Green Mountain Boys captured Fort Ticonderoga, across Lake Champlain in New York. A year later the Americans had strengthened the fort and expanded it to Mount Independence, in Orwell, Vermont, by building a floating bridge across the lake.

In 1777, though, a massive force of British seasoned Regulars moved south from Canada to overwhelm both Fort Ticonderoga and Mount Independence. To save his troops, American general Arthur St. Clair ordered the vastly outnumbered Americans to withdraw to the southeast. While the main force continued on, a rearguard of 1,000 men dug in at Hubbardton to slow down the Redcoats and their German allies. This led to the only Revolutionary War battle fought entirely on Vermont soil.

Although technically the Battle of Hubbardton was considered an American defeat, it accomplished what it was intended to do. So many casualties were inflicted on the British that they finally gave up. It was partially because of this bold stand that British general John Burgoyne said of the people of Vermont: "They are the most active and most rebellious race on the continent."

The 255-acre historical site includes trails leading to various stages of the battle. A visitors' center houses a museum with period artifacts and a large fiber optic map and accompanying narration of the battle stages.

Directions: Take U.S. Route 4 east from Rutland to exit 4, and then go north 7 miles to East Hubbardton. The battle site is on the left at 5696 Monument Road. The site is open late May through mid-October, Thursday–Sunday, 9:30 a.m.–5:00 p.m. For a complete account of the Battle of Hubbardton or more information about the site, see: http://historicvermont.org/hubbardton/ hubbardton.html or call (802) 759-2412.

YOUTUBE VIDEO
"The Battle of Hubbardton Animated Map (6:24) 🍁

MATTHEW LYON—ELECTED TO CONGRESS FROM JAIL

Fair Haven

To clarify the plaque's wording, Lyon was jailed for violating the Sedition Act, true. But that act was declared unconstitutional a year later, which freed him.

The village green plaque pictured here just hints at Matthew Lyon's remarkable life and his contributions to early Vermont. Here's a little bit more of the story.

After attending school and beginning to learn the printing trade in his native Ireland, Matthew Lyon had guts enough to sail to America as an indentured servant at the age of fifteen. He first worked on a farm in Woodbury, Connecticut, and then moved to Wallingford, Vermont, where he gained his independence. During the Revolution, Lyon was commissioned as a lieutenant with Ethan Allen and the Green Mountain Boys and helped capture Fort Ticonderoga.

Lyon became wealthy after the Revolutionary War by learning how to make paper from wood pulp. He founded the village of Fair Haven and created the *Fair Haven Gazette*, a weekly for which he served as both editor and publisher. The *Gazette* gave Lyon a chance to express his strong pro-Jefferson views at the expense of John Adams, whom he viewed as a monarchist.

Lyon's influence helped elect him to Congress in 1796, where he wielded even more influence, even if by somewhat unconventional methods. On one occasion he spit on Federalist congressman Roger Griswold for insults against him having to do with his anti-Adams position. Griswold attacked him with his cane, but Lyon was able to get to the House fireplace, where he grabbed a poker and gave Griswold a nasty pasting.

In 1798 Lyon was convicted and sentenced to four months in jail and fined $1,000 for violating the Sedition Act, signed by President Adams and making it unlawful for an American to defame a president. Even so, he easily won reelection despite being in jail at voting time. The Green Mountain Boys threatened to retaliate by destroying the jail, but Lyon successfully urged peaceful resistance. A year later the Sedition Act was declared unconstitutional, and in 1800 Matthew Lyon was able to cast the deciding presidential vote for his hero, Thomas Jefferson, in a runoff after an electoral college deadlock.

Lyon, his wife, and twelve children then moved to Kentucky, where he successfully ran for Congress once more. When Lyon moved again to Arkansas, he failed to become a congressman from a third state, but not because he was not successful in his campaign. Actually, he was elected, but died before he could take a seat there. In 1840, Congress refunded the $1,000 he was fined after his Imprisonment for sedition, plus expenses and Interest. What a man! What a life!

Directions: Fair Haven is 12 miles west of Rutland on U.S. Route 4. Take exit 2 south to get to the center of town. For more information please visit www.fairhavenvt.org. ❧

GIANT ELEPHANTS . . . ONCE ROAMED . . . IN VERMONT. YES!

Mount Holly

credit: Flying Puffin (CC BY-SA 2.0)

Fossil finds greatly aid paleontologists in establishing written history.

Well, "giant" in the sense that they weighed twice as much as elephants living today and stood about 12-feet tall on all fours. Depending on whose opinion you accept, the woolly mammoth began grazing about 11,000 years ago, several thousand years after the ice retreated and grasslands reestablished themselves in the meadows of what is now Vermont. These large mammals chewed grass and leaves with eight-pound molars. These were low-tech tools that yielded high-volume greens mastication. They were essential, though. It takes a heap o' fuel to keep a five-ton woolly mammoth happy—or ambulatory, at the very least.

A Swiss zoologist named Louis Agassiz proved to be instrumental in our understanding of what life was like in the Ice Age, among other things. In 1848, two years after he came to the United States—Harvard professorship in hand—Agassiz received tangible validation of a part of his theory. Workmen in Mount Holly, building a railroad from Bellows Falls to Rutland, uncovered the remains of a woolly mammoth from what were the mud layers of an ancient swamp, 11 feet below the surface. Most of the bones were taken by the workmen, but, as written in the *Vermont Semi-Weekly Record* in September 5, 1865, "the most perfect tusk was secured by Prof. Zadock Thompson and is lodged in the State Cabinet at Montpelier. This tusk was 80 inches long and four inches in diameter. The molar tooth, now in the possession of Prof. Agassiz, weighs eight pounds and presents a grinding surface of eight inches long and four broad. A plaster cast of it is on exhibition with the tusk at our State Cabinet."

Seventeen years later, near Brattleboro about 30 miles to the south, laborer James Morse was similarly mucking about on Daniel Pratt's farm and found the tusk of a young mammoth, about half the size of the Mount Holly specimen. The *Vermont Semi-Weekly Record* duly recorded this event as well: "The workman on discovering it took a piece to Mr. Pratt, remarking as he handed it to him, that he had found a curious piece of wood. Mr. Pratt on looking at it discovered its true nature." Thank you, Messrs Morse and Pratt.

Directions: The fossil tusk of the young woolly mammoth can be seen on the third floor of the Brooks Memorial Library (near the elevator), at 324 Main Street, Brattleboro. Call (802) 254-5290 or visit www.brooks.lib.vt.us for more information. A plaster cast of the full-sized mammoth molar can be seen at the Perkins Geology Museum, University of Vermont, 180 Colchester Avenue, Burlington. Call (802) 656-8694 or visit www.uvm.edu/perkins for additional information. (What happened to the original tusk is a mystery.) ✤

Is Vermont's Most Beautiful Castle Haunted?

Proctor

One classy destination at Wilson Castle is the French Renaissance Room. The round window you see is hand painted. On the table is a statue of the moon goddess Helena.

Visitors come from all over the globe. "Guests from France said they had never seen anything like this—*in France,*" says docent coordinator Sheila Kelley of the Wilson Castle. What they see is a thirty-two-room, thirteen-fireplace brick structure built in the manner of a Flemish castle, with many arches breaking up the overall straight lines, but designed in a mix of architectural styles, to give the original owner the illusion of visiting a different country when leaving one room and entering another. Queen Anne (along with a tea set from the *Queen Mary*), Scottish baronial, Dutch neo-renaissance, and Romanesque revival—they're all here.

Vermont-born Dr. John Johnson convinced his English bride to fund the castle's construction (and he's not available to tell us just how he got away with that), completed in 1874 at a cost of $1.3 million. Wife Sarah Johnson insisted that all the brick be imported from England, which today is causing a few structural problems because of the slightly warmer climate for which the brick was fabricated. When Sarah died a few years after the castle's completion, it was repossessed and sold. In 1939, radio pioneer Herbert Wilson bought the 115-acre estate and created another radio station on the property. (The 100-foot tower still stands, although I found no bandwidth trace of the "still operating" WEWE-AM.)

Wilson joined the Signal Corps in World War II and retired a colonel. He died in 1981 and left the estate to his daughter, who manages it today with *her* daughter.

Sheila's favorite areas are the stairways and the turret. Other popular spots Include the eight-sided music room, containing some of the castle's eighty-six stained glass windows, a beautiful fireplace, and an organ. About a third of the way up the wall is a French cherry wainscoting, above which is what looks like wallpaper but is actually a complex, hand-stenciled design, identical to that of the ceiling, which, we are told, took four and a half years to complete.

The Johnsons, and for the first couple of years the Wilsons, maintained an aviary, including a flock of peacocks that roamed the property. But the harsh Vermont winters and the ample local population of foxes, obviously finding the peacocks extremely tasty, made this a short-lived conceit.

But let's get to the title of this story. Sheila, who replaced Levi Nelson as top guide, says there's no question that what Levi told her when she first started working here—that Wilson Castle was haunted—*definitely* is true. She says that her experiences over the past six years have fully convinced her that spirits from the Johnson family (and or maybe the Wilsons, as well) regularly come to call. Levi found evidences of strange occurrences between his departure time from work on an early evening to his return the next morning. To this, Sheila can add personal accounts both heard and seen.

"My very first experience," she begins, "was hearing a man's voice call out 'Hello' twice from downstairs (I was on the second floor), and then going down to find no one there.

"But it was the second year that things got a bit crazy," Sheila said. "My daughter had just brought me an iced coffee I had asked for after telling her I'd be here alone all day. When she arrived she said, 'Mom, I thought you were working alone today.'

"'I am,' I said.'

"'Oh. Are you giving a tour?'

"'No, I'm not.'

"'Then who's the lady upstairs in the window?'

"After looking at each other with some unease, we walked upstairs to the bedroom above the driveway. The window my daughter had pointed out was empty, but for some reason I felt drawn to the closed closet door. I opened it to find an empty space—except for a dress on a hanger, dark blue with a white collar. When I turned to look at my daughter, her face was drained of color.

"'What's wrong, Honey? You're scaring me.'

"'You don't understand, Mom. That's the dress the lady was wearing who looked at me from the window!'

"We were both speechless. And just a few days later, I read in a book about the castle on a table in the library that a woman was frequently seen wearing the same dress that had been hanging in the closet. Just last year a tourist saw that same woman in the window in a picture he took in front of the castle. A little later in the year, another tourist saw her as well. Yes, she certainly gets around!

"There were multiple witnesses to another paranormal event a couple of years later. I was giving a tour in the dining room, and a stack of plates on the table began to vibrate. After a minute or two the tourists looked at me, not sure that I wasn't the one making them shake—but I was just as surprised as they were.

"Also, bells seem to go off a lot—once when I was with a couple and leaving the grandmother's bedroom (where the blue dress hangs in the closet), which everyone now wants to see.

"Another time after one of the late-night Haunted Tours, my

daughter and I were the only ones left in the castle. It was after 11 o'clock. She was in the art gallery and I was on the veranda. I heard her call me in a frightened way and went to her. When I reached the gallery, I heard two notes on the piano. It was then she was able to tell me she heard a man and a woman talking in the front of the castle. When we investigated, no one was there.

"Probably the most bizarre experience of all was when I led a French family tour. They were talking among themselves, and on the way downstairs, when all of a sudden I could understand everything they were saying—In French, even though *I don't know French—and I even answered them!*"

Sheila's guess is that the spirits are for the most part friendly. As for the Lady in Blue, most tend to identify her as the ghost of Sarah Johnson. Author David Pritkin corroborates this in his book *New England Ghosts* (See Bibliography, p. 229.), and refers to her as "Lady Johnson." As part of his research Pitkin interviewed a number of guides—at the castle and at other sites said to be spirit-occupied—and advised them to "just acknowledge the ghosts. Tell them you know they're there. Ask them to cut out the pranks and just let you do your job."

Says Sheila: "No actions seem to have been directed toward me. I like my job here. As Levi used to say, 'until I see my name written on the wall in blood, I don't think I'll need to take a day off.'" She is sensitive to feeling Sarah's presence, and to experiencing different feelings that are not her own. Sheila, in fact, has become as close to a professional spirit watcher as one can be. If you have a paranormal experience or two you'd like to share, contact her at ghostgirl6@icloud.com.

Directions: Off the Rutland Bypass, U.S. Route 4, take exit 6. Turn left 2 1/2 miles from West Rutland on West Proctor Road. Tours run daily from late May until late October, 9:00 a.m. to 6:00 p.m., the last tour starting at 5:30 p.m. For more information visit www.wilsoncastle.com or call (802) 773-3284.

YOUTUBE VIDEO:
"A Look at Wilson Castle in Rutland, VT (1:10)
(Short, but dramatic tour by drone) ❧

BILL COULD USE A LITTLE HELP

Proctor

That's completed plaster Bill on the left, and marble Bill-to-be on the right. If the museum doesn't find money enough to finish the job, the two may look like this for a long time.

Going through the Hall of Presidents exhibit at the Vermont Marble Museum, it's hard not to notice that the two walls of bas-reliefs end with President George H. W. Bush. The two presidents succeeding him are missing. Is this a matter of laxity, or could this be a political statement of some kind?

I'm not sure. But let's take matters in sequence. Around 1995 or so, according to Proctor sculptor Brent Wilson, he was asked to add President Bill Clinton to the second row during that president's first term. But the museum wasn't able to meet his asking price, and the project was scrapped.

Fast forward to 2002. Local sculptor Vince Forte is commissioned to do a full bust of Clinton. Why a full bust? Well, the two side walls are full of presidents, and what remains is space for another row down the middle of the gallery. These will be three-dimensional busts instead of bas-reliefs, because they will be viewed from all sides rather than faces just protruding from marble slabs anchored to the wall.

Before he died in 2004, Forte had completed a plaster bust and was well into work on the final marble version. Again, Brent Wilson was asked to step into the breach. His preference would have been to sculpt a bas-relief, but alas, that decision had been set in stone. Wilson told Robert Pye, director of the museum, how much money he would require to finish the piece but had not been given a go-ahead at this writing. "We need to get the money, because it is an expensive deal," Pye told the *Rutland Herald.*

About that time Bill Clinton was in the area, giving a commencement address at Middlebury College. Museum officials invited him to drop over to Proctor to take a look at the work in progress, but he was a no-show. Whether he was concerned about being hit up to cover some of the cost of completing his own bust is not known.

Making three phone calls to get permission for us to photograph the subject of this story, gift-shop associate Rob Hodge took us to the basement, opened a couple of locked doors, and removed several of layers of plastic wrap so we could see both Bill in the plaster-flesh and his marble twin-to-be. When finished, FYI, he will look jovial, with a slight gap between his two upper incisors. At this time, however, staffer Linda Doty recently told me, the President Clinton bust is still unfinished. It has made it upstairs, however, but not in the Hall of Presidents. It can be found awaiting completion in the Sample Room on the south side of the museum. Things could move quickly, though. Ask for an update while you're there.

Incidentally, both the Marble Museum men's room and ladies' room were 2007 finalists for the honor of "best bathroom in the country." (Can you imagine how many judges that must have taken?) There were five finalists, with no clue as to the rankings from two to five, but hey, at worst, who wouldn't settle for having the fifth best bathroom in the country? (And if they each received a vote, this is almost as good as the top prize.)

Directions: Once in Proctor, head west going over the marble bridge (You were expecting, maybe, reinforced concrete?), past the Proctor library, and then turn north at the intersection. The museum is on the right. Said to be the largest of its kind in the world, the Vermont Marble Museum is open daily from mid-May until the end of October, 10:00 a.m. to 5:00 p.m. For more information visit www.vermont-marble.com or call (800) 427-1396. ❦

WHO CASHED SOCIAL SECURITY CHECK 00-000-001?

Rutland

When Ida May Fuller dropped by the Rutland Social Security office on November 4, 1939, morning, she knew she had been paying for something called social security for her three years of work as a teacher. "It wasn't that I expected anything, mind you," she said later. "I just knew that I had been paying for it and I wanted to ask the people in Rutland about it."

Ida May's claim was taken by claims clerk Elizabeth Corcoran Burke and transmitted to the Claims Division in Washington, D.C., for adjudication. The case was reviewed and sent to the Treasury Department for payment in January 1940. The claims were grouped in batches of 1,000 and a certification list for each batch was sent to the Treasury. Miss Fuller's claim was first on the certification list, so she was issued the first social security check: number 00-000-001, dated January 31, 1940, in the amount of $22.54. This was her first retirement check, which she received at age sixty-five. Over the next thirty-five years, until she died at age one hundred, Ida May received a total of $22,888.92 in social security benefits.

JOHN DEERE, FORGOTTEN NATIVE SON

Rutland

The 5.2-acre John Deere Historic Site contains an archeological site, Deere's home, his blacksmith shop, and a gift shop. It is located in Grand Detour, Illinois. A plaque above the site of the shop in which John Deere apprenticed as a blacksmith stands in

Rmherman (CC BY-SA 4.0)

The steel plow revolutionized farming worldwide when John Deere first used cast steel, instead of iron, to turn the soil. The advantage: It cut through sticky soil without clogging.

Middlebury, Vermont. But in Rutland, Vermont, the birthplace of John Deere, no statue, monument, or plaque exists to tell you so. The closest the town comes by way of commemoration is a copy of *John Deere's Company: A History of Deere & Company and Its Times*, donated to the Rutland Historical Society by a John Deere great-grandsomething. It is not prominently displayed.

This is not to say that the inventor of the steel plow, which revolutionized U.S. farming—and eventually worldwide farming as well—is not on the minds of Rutland residents. A local group is trying to raise money for a bike path to be named after Deere but is having funding difficulties. (It asked the John Deere Foundation for $120,000 but was turned down.)

It could be that Rutland has been slow coming on board with a public display of affection because John Deere didn't accomplish much before he left the state at age two. Illinois is reaping all of the rewards—both in fame and fortune—that Deere and his company had to bestow, because that's where the man spent most of his productive years. Middlebury basks in a bit of reflected glory, because at least Deere learned the blacksmith trade there before moving on to greater things in the Prairie State. Yes, that would call for at least a plaque.

This has to hurt a little bit in Rutland. For all these years the question probably has been: "Why do we reward a resident who skipped town for good before he even went to school here?" and now it's "*How* do we reward a resident who skipped town for good before he even went to school here?" You can see the conflict in their minds. The same thing happened to Rudy Vallee. He left Island Pond when he was a toddler, and scant signs of his Vermont presence remain. The town of Sharon, on the other hand, has a statue to Joseph Smith, who brought Mormonism and the Angel Moroni to the world, and he was taken off to Palmyra, New York, before his first Vermont birthday. So it's a very tricky decision. We wish the citizens of Rutland well as they sort through the pros and cons. ♣

BIG WIND AT GRANDPA'S KNOB

Things don't always go as well as they might locating Vermont (Who Knew?-worthy) topics. Example: One day we were looking for signs of a historic wind energy-development project installed in 1941 at Grandpa's Knob, the first large-scale electricity-producing windmill in the United States, and world's largest at the time.

One thousand Central Vermont customers were the world's first to have their homes and businesses powered by wind. This was to be the pioneer program for a renewable energy industry that nearly a century later is still getting off the ground.

The site was a 1,976-foot mountaintop between West Rutland and Castleton. General Electric and several partners took on this colossal effort—consisting of a 240-ton base and two 75-foot-by-11-foot blades, each weighing eight tons. The blades churned out electricity in 70-mile-per-hour winds, handling gusts of 115 miles per hour. When a main bearing failed in 1943, though, wind generation halted completely. Repairing It during World War II was unthinkable, and a replacement took more than two years to manufacture and install.

This I knew (but not, inexplicably, what I *should* have known) when I visited the Castleton town manager.

"Can you tell me how to get to Grandpa's Knob?" I asked administrative assistant at the time Jill Potter.

"Well, yes," she said and hesitated. "What are you looking for, specifically?"

I told her we wanted to photograph the windmill bringing electricity to the Castleton area. Jill said there wasn't much up there to see. "That site was razed in 1946," said (now former) town manager Jon Dodd, just walking into the room.

It was then I realized that the subject of our photo shoot had not existed for more than seventy years. What I missed was that after the part had been installed on March 3, 1945 with no problem, it worked without incident until one of the blades snapped off March 26, flying 700 feet down the mountain slope. Engineers expressed confidence that repairs would begin immediately, but in wartime steel was a luxury. This, plus the fact that coal was then 20 percent cheaper than wind-produced electricity, meant that dismantling the project was inevitable.

Still, in the end, the wind turbine on Grandpa's Knob was considered an engineering success, and helped scientists understand the behavior of the wind. It also helped improve wind turbine technology and proved that wind could be used to generate electricity. So why wouldn't a new Grandpa's Knob windmill or two work even better with today's technology? GE? Budd Company? Anybody?

Regardless, Town Manager Dodd was not going to let me get away with such shoddy research. "So good luck to you, Don Quixote," he said as we left. He paused. "You know, 'tilting at windmills'?"

"Yes, I hear what you're saying," I said. "No need to explain."

"You never know," said Jon.

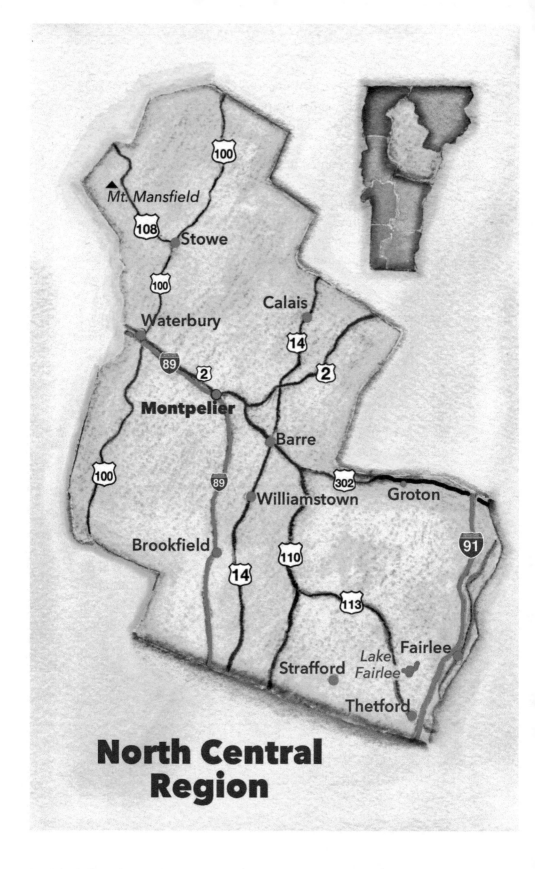

North Central
Region

6

NORTH CENTRAL

If you've ever looked through The New Yorker *magazine—or for that matter* Time, Sports Illustrated, Esquire, The New York Times, *and a few others, you're bound to have seen Ed Koren's huggable furry cartoon creatures—but with a bite! They have points of view, and love nothing more than sharing them. Their creator, meantime, is on call 24 hours a day for the Brookfield Volunteer Fire Department, giving back to the community as well as to the hundreds of thousands of readers who have enjoyed his work over the last half-century.*

Millions of people have seen The Sound of Music *over the years—either the movie or the stage musical. Few know, though, that the Trapp Family Singers never sang "Do-Re-Mi," "Sixteen Going on Seventeen," or "My Favorite Things." Actually, they sang very little in English, mostly in Italian and German. The movie songs were written by Richard Rodgers and Oscar Hammerstein for the actors who sang them. Included is a memorial tribute to Maria von Trapp, who died at age 99 after a life of giving to others.*

Some ice cream flavors seem to be naturals. Others just don't quite make it. Ben & Jerry's, founded by two boys in Burlington, Vermont, back in 1978, push the envelope when it comes to flavor naming. The wackier the better. Do you remember Honey I'm Home, Economic Crunch, Sugar Plum, or Ethan Almond? Me either. The boys are good, but sometimes they try just a tad too hard at the naming game. For enough groan-inducing ice cream flavor puns to last you a lifetime, be sure to read the tombstones at the Flavor Graveyard in Waterbury.

5,000 MILES OF SNOWMOBILE TRAILS—
THAT'S VAST

Barre

Credit: VAST

VAST's 27,000 members depend on 8,000 Vermont private property owners to allow snowmobilers to use their land—part of the 5,000 miles of trails to be enjoyed each winter

Keep in mind this is a teeny state. So it's unusual enough for there to be nearly 5,000 miles of snowmobile trails crisscrossing its meadows, forests, mountains, and valleys. But Vermont is also the only New England state with interconnecting trails that not only provide access through one another, but also reach beyond the state's borders into Massachusetts, Quebec, New York, and New Hampshire. Seven customs entry points connect Vermont and Quebec trails alone.

Alexis Nowak, former trails administrator for VAST—the Vermont Association of Snowmobile Travelers—walked me through the various networks crucial to making all of this happen. "These trails are all maintained by the 138 local VAST clubs, which are responsible for all grooming, trail construction, and repair during the off-season. Each club has a contract with VAST to groom the trails twice a week during our sixteen-week season [December 16 to April 15], and we reimburse them for each mile groomed. The clubs send me a grooming log sheet weekly."

Growing up in Buffalo, New York, Alexis had been a snowmobiler since childhood, so no drastic lifestyle changes were necessary when she joined VAST in resources management, which led to a job in the U.S. Forest Service as a hydrologic technician and later as a GPS consultant mapping wetlands.

"Eight thousand private-property owners allow us on their land," said Alexis. "The relationships we maintain with them are key to our success. We try to keep communications open, and the clubs in turn host landowner appreciation dinners, stack wood, maybe give gifts, whatever seems appropriate." A few agencies that manage public lands provide access as well, such as the U.S. Forest Service, the Agency of Natural Resources, and the U.S. Fish and Wildlife Service.

Then there are the 27,000 members, whose registration and trail passes provide VAST with its principal sources of revenue. Several years ago, membership stood at a high of 42,000. Alexis believes, however, that two recent phenomena—warmer winters and mandatory liability insurance—have resulted in the falloff.

The most exciting project in work is the conversion of the 96-mile Lamoille Valley Rail Trail to a four-season multiuse recreation path. VAST recently signed a contract with the Vermont Agency of Transportation to manage the estimated ten-year, $7 million project, which will stretch through Franklin, Lamoille, and Caledonia Counties. "Senator Sanders was instrumental in securing a $5 million high-priority grant for this project through the Highway Administration," said Alexis. "We're very fortunate."

For more information about VAST or the trails it maintains, visit www.vtvast.org. ❦

THE ROCK OF AGES MEETS STAR TREK!

Barre

Some call it Graniteville; others call it the Rock of Ages. But whatever you call it, this is one big hole. To be precise, at 600 feet deep it is the largest deep-hole granite quarry in the world. Todd Paton is senior among the guides who conduct narrated tours from the visitors' center to the quarry. He's also director of tourism and visitor services. "We see between 55,000 and 65,000 visitors each [six-month] season," he says.

Todd offers to take us on a personal tour of the quarry, just behind the shuttle bus pulling out of the parking lot. During an interim stop at the granite bowling alley (result: gutter ball), Todd says: "They thought they'd have a big turnaround with these granite bowling alleys, but the bowling balls couldn't take it!" Kids have fun trying it out, though.

But what does this all have to do with Star Wars? you ask. You'll find out a few paragraphs from now. First, a bit of context.

We reach the fenced-off quarry itself moments later, where decades ago a derrick just to the left, a little yellow cage it transported, called a rider box, lowered men down to the bottom every day. The derricks were all run electrically, and if you looked about 50 yards behind each of them, you'd see a red building with white trim. That's where the derrick operator sat to run the derricks. Now from where he was, it was impossible to see the bottom of the quarry. And from where we're standing, *we* can't see the bottom of the quarry either. So we had a signalman who sat in or near that little red shack right on the edge of the quarry wall. He relayed hand signals to the derrick operator, and that's how we ran our derricks. Because of the loud noise from the drilling, we were unable to communicate with walkie-talkies. So everything was done through hand signals.

The number of people employed in the granite industry in and around Barre has shrunk to half the 3,000 who worked here in the mid- and late-twentieth century. The number of imported headstones from China and India increased by the year. Although the quality of the imported stones was poor, labor costs ware so low in China that manufacturers could sell them for a fraction of the price paid for U.S.-made stones. That's still the case today.

The visitors' center can do nothing about this, of course, but the company can add attractions to get visitor numbers back up where they once were.

Oh yes—Star Trek. You've been very patient, so here's the story. In this age of digital photography and filmmaking, things aren't always what they seem. In 2008, Paramount Pictures was planning the eleventh of the thirteen Star Trek movies—one of the few without a sub-title. The producers needed a sheer cliff to add more drama to a car-chase scene featuring a teen-age version of Capt. James T. Kirk. What better location than the 600-foot cliff at the Rock of Ages quarry. Although the actors didn't come within 3,000 miles of Barre, Todd said the action and dialog were digitally inserted in footage shot at the quarry the previous year. We won't spoil the ending for you. It all plays out In the two-minute-eleven-second Star Trek trailer you can access below.

Directions: Take exit 6 on Interstate 89. Follow Route 63 to the bottom of the hill. At the traffic light, follow the signs to Graniteville/Graniteville Quarries. Go straight up Middle Hill Road. About 200 feet past Lazy Lion Campground will be the driveway for the Rock of Ages on the left at 558 Graniteville Road. The visitors' center hours vary by season. For more information visit www.rockofages.com or call (802) 476-3119.

YOUTUBE VIDEOS
Video Descent into Rock of Ages Quarry (:58)
"Star Trek (2009) - Trailer 1 HD" (2:11) 🍁

"A Folly"

Brookfield

**A Folly, formerly the Caroline, is a memorial to Vance and
Al's dear friend Tommy Gillette.**

if you're returning to I-89 exit 4, you'll see a nautical curiosity on
the south side of town. At the end of a dock across the road from
the house at 408 Ridge Road is a Downeast lobster boat, serenely
bobbing—or seemingly so—at the lowest of ebb tides: two acres
of lawn.

A Folly, owned by Al Wilker and his wife, Vance Smith, wasn't
always the name of the boat. Al was halfway into the refurbishing
of *Caroline,* as the lobster boat was known back then, when their
good friend Tommy Gillette died—"Much too early," says Vance. So
before life passed them by, they chucked it all and bought a 36-foot
sailboat. For the next few years they spent a lot of time tooling
around Lake Champlain and then came back to decide what to
do with *Caroline,* which had been sitting in the barn all that time.

Then it came to them. First they built the dock. Then they towed
Caroline across the street and down the hill. Then they renamed her

A Folly, which perfectly matches the whimsical English definition often applied to formal gardens: "An architectural construction that isn't what it appears to be."

Says Vance, "It's a memorial to Tommy Gillette, to getting the most out of life when you can. And sometimes, in the right light and after a few beers, you can see whitecaps."

Directions: From I-89 South, take exit 4. On Route 66, go east 1 mile to Randolph Center, and turn north. One mile farther, where Route 66 makes a sharp right, go left onto Ridge Road. *A Folly* is across the street from 408 Ridge Road. ❦

Pairing Artistry with Public Service

Brookfield

When I called Edward Koren to arrange a day and time to talk about his profession as an author and longtime cartoonist for *The New Yorker*, he agreed—with one request: "Give me your cell phone number in case there's a fire."

Ed has been a member of Brookfield's Volunteer Fire Department for the past 29 years and is certified for cardiopulmonary resuscitation (CPR) and other essential emergency techniques. He's on call 24 hours a day. "But at age 81," he says, "it seems I'm relegated more and more to traffic duty!" Along with his fellow volunteers, Ed answers about 25 alarms each year, driving to each incident in his own car (roof-top red warning light activated) after changing into his protective gear.

We sat on the patio of a flagstone-terraced backyard behind his farmhouse, just a block or so from the town's floating bridge—a space filled with a variety of trees, shrubs, and flowers, plus a purple yurt on the top level, outfitted for visiting grandchildren.

When Ed Koren was a freshman at Columbia University he began submitting cartoons to *The Jester,* the school's humor magazine. By the time he was a senior he was also the magazine's editor. His big break came when a classmate's family friend introduced him to the then art editor of *The New Yorker,* where he began submitting his work.

At his Brookfield workspace, Ed Koren has produced most of the 1,000-plus *New Yorker* cartoons and 28 covers drawn over more than half a century.

Before becoming a regular contributor at that publication, though, Ed did what most twenty-somethings did—and still do, under such circumstances—experiment. In his case it was working in several six-month to year-and-a-half increments, as first an urban planner; then an intern with a prominent Paris print studio; and finally, as a U.S Army enlisted man. (In that last assignment, in a single day at Fort Dix in 1960, he was fortunate enough to not only witness Elvis Presley's discharge, but meet another enlisted man —the future *News Yorker* writer Calvin Trillin—who remains a friend to this day.)

Those familiar with Ed's magazine cartoons enjoy a universe inhabited by furry, mild-mannered yet iconoclastic vertebrates, whose observations of the population around them are by turns whimsical or penetrating, and frequently illuminate the subtle contradictions and hypocrisies that surround both them and all the rest of us.

Every Monday or Tuesday, after a week of coming up with ideas, then either keeping or discarding them, Ed draws illustrations and writes captions for the best half-dozen or so, then scans his finished products into the computer and sends them off for viewing by his editor.

"There are plenty of ideas," he says, "but only a minute percentage of them are published—and those few are hard-won—this is true for all of us, by the way." Occasionally Ed is able to slightly alter a rejected entry and make it stick the second time around. "But it's *still* only a minute percentage," he adds. Coming from a man who has published well over a thousand cartoons—including 28 covers—in *The New Yorker* since 1962, this may be difficult to believe. But Ed would emphasize for perspective's sake that his enviable record has been accomplished over a half century—and then some. (A partial list of other publications in which his work has appeared includes *The New York Times, Esquire, Sports Illustrated, Vanity Fair, Fortune,* and *Time.*)

Although Ed's Furry People continue to evolve, as they have in subtle ways over the past decades, he has no plans to introduce others. "What you see is what I'm going to be doing until I can't do it anymore," he says. "You could call me a first responder doing CPR on our screwed-up society. I think Lily Tomlin said it best: "No matter how cynical I get, I can never keep up.""

YouTube Video:
"Edward Koren: The Capricious Line" (5:47)
(Ed goes back to his roots at Columbia) ❦

Morey's Steamboat—Was Fulton a Fraud?

Fairlee

Most history books credit Robert Fulton's *Clermont* with making the first successful steamboat trip in 1807. True, Fulton's Hudson River voyage from New York City to Albany was the first commercial steamboat service in the world.

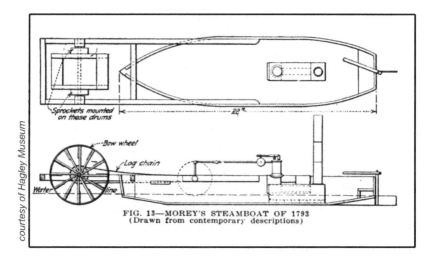

courtesy of Hagley Museum

FIG. 13—MOREY'S STEAMBOAT OF 1793
(Drawn from contemporary descriptions)

If Fulton started out so badly—poor design, bad planning, internal bickering—why did he come off so well in the history books? Answer: Follow the money. Fulton struck a better financial deal than Morey.

Gould's History of River Navigation, however, describes the voyage not as a success, but as a disaster. "The rudder had so little power that the vessel could hardly be managed. The spray from the wheels dashed over the passengers." The skippers of other river craft took advantage of the *Clermont's* unwieldiness, and cut in front of her to save time.

As a result, the *Clermont* was completely rebuilt and tried again the following May, with Fulton himself aboard. The voyage got off to a bad start by leaving several passengers behind when the ship made an uncharacteristic on-time departure. Even so, a leaky boiler was the only problem on the upriver voyage. On the passage back down the Hudson, though, there were more leaks. According to Gould, "After fifty-seven hours of struggling, the engine ceased to work." The boat grounded, with Captain Wesswell blaming the pilot and the pilot blaming the captain. This led "to a torrent of vituperation on each side, [as well as] blows, in which one of the parties was knocked down, and one received a black eye." Another successful voyage!

But here's the kicker: The *Clermont* was not the first, but the *twelfth* steamboat to be built and become a part of river traffic in the nineteenth century. Anachronism aside, today we might be calling this fiasco Fultongate!

In 1792, fifteen years earlier, Fairlee, Vermont inventor Samuel Morey built a steamboat with a paddle-wheel in the prow. One Sunday he and an assistant, John Mann, made their first trip across the Connecticut River and back from Orford, New Hampshire, to Fairlee. A few years later, Morey constructed a new and improved version, with paddle-wheels on each side for more speed and better stability. He sailed from Bradenton, New Jersey, to Philadelphia on the Delaware River, where his newly christened *Aunt Sally* was publicly exhibited. Fulton and Morey were aware of each other's efforts as early as 1793, and the race was on for the funding that would assure commercial success.

Enter Robert R. Livingston, chancellor of New York State, a wealthy entrepreneur, and an inventor as well. Before meeting Fulton, Livingston took a ride in Morey's steamboat and offered to back him in a joint venture, but Morey refused when Livingston insisted on too large a percentage of the proceeds. Livingston then went to Fulton, and the deal that resulted is what eventually made its way into the history books. When Morey heard about it, he is said to have scuttled the *Aunt Sally* in what is now Lake Morey.

But Samuel Morey, holder of a number of patents, also designed and built the Bellows Falls Canal in 1802. (See Chapter 2). So it's not as though he would have brooded rudderless after getting the shaft from Fulton and Livingston.

Fairlee is located off Exit 15 on I-91 north; http://www.ctrivertravel.net/fairlee.htm.

YOUTUBE VIDEO:
"Samuel Morey PBS" (17:27)
(A search for the "Aunt Sally") ❦

WALKING THE NATION'S SMALLEST CAPITAL

Montpelier

**Vermont's beautiful State House was the first commercial
building to be constructed from Barre granite.
(And yes, that's real gold on the dome.)**

Just a few miles south of exit 8 on I-89, the tableau of green valleys,
farms, and hills spread out below make a highway warrior feel more
like a Piper Cub pilot on the last approach before putting down.
On your right is the city of Montpelier, home of fewer than 8,000
souls, with the population swelling to nearly 8,200 when the legislature is in session (representatives plus assistants, press, lobbyists,
and assorted hangers-on). Just off the exit you can see the golden
dome. Now there's proof you're in a capital city.

If the legislature isn't in session, you'll have a good shot at a
parking spot near the capitol building. If so, walk in the front
door and take a tour if you'd like. When you're ready, walk out the
other side to a trail that leads straight to 185-acre Hubbard Park.
Here you'll find wooded stands of oak, beech, pine, and hemlock,

dotted with picnic areas, a pond, hiking trails, and a 54-foot stone observation tower.

An alternative is to walk back out the capitol front door and left down State Street 1 block to the Vermont Historical Society Museum. After you browse a bit, ask one of the informed and accommodating docents the best way to spend the next couple of hours (or days) in the nation's smallest capital. Bring a map to check off likely destinations. She'll (there've been only ladies on duty the times I've visited) tell you where to pick up a four-color pictograph map of the downtown area (the one with the buildings labeled), so you can sit on a bench with a cup of coffee and plan a route tailored specifically to your interests, depending on the length of your stay.

Directions: For capitol tour information visit www.vtstatehouse. org or call (802) 828-0386; for more information about the smallest capital, visit www.montpelier-vt.org

YouTube Video:
"Montpelier, Vermont Farmers' Market 2014 - Walk Through" (3:30) 🍁

Six Feet Under Is Not the Only Way to Go

Cemetery management in the twenty-first century is developing its own set of issues. "The baby boomers want options," says Montpelier's Green Mount Cemetery superintendent Patrick Healy. "They do not want to be told 'either it's this or it's nothing.' They'll go someplace else. So we're trying to go with the times.

"For one thing, there's much more cremation going on today. Up in an older part of the cemetery is a section that hasn't been used since we bought the place in 1854. It's all ledge [a shelf of rock] 6 inches below the surface. So what we do is sell plots about 3½ by 11 feet wide. We drill cores [Patrick shows me a copper/bronze casing about 3 feet long by 3 inches in diameter] the way rock is prepared before being blasted to carve out a freeway. We can put a monument there, because all you have to do is pour a little bit of concrete on the ledge itself, pin it, and when 'your time' comes, we just unscrew the cap on the casing, take a funnel, pour you in it—and you're home."

"But what if you're claustrophobic?"

"I haven't heard a complaint yet," says Patrick.

"We have another section called Woodland Gardens. It's not big, but there are some paths through the woods. It's not your traditional 'mow the lawn' area. What we found was that a lot of people were spreading their relatives' cremated remains out in nature—in the Atlantic Ocean, Florida, or a favorite fishing spot—but they still wanted a place to come and remember. The stones are flush to the ground, so nature is disrupted only slightly." Strange as it seems, cemeteries now are in competition and have to figure out how to market their services. "I'll probably be doing commercials on WDEV before long!" says Patrick.

THE MORSE BROTHERS, CRACKER-BARREL PHILOSOPHERS EXTRAORDINAIRE

Montpelier

We'd heard about Burr Morse–his farm, his eight-generation maple sugaring operation, his farm store, his wit and wisdom. But when I told Burr about *Vermont . . . Who Knew?* and wanted to hear a couple of the stories that had made him famous, Burr backed off a bit.

"I've got a monthly column to write," he said. "My second book will be coming out soon." I had the feeling Burr needed that material for his own projects and was leery of diluting his brand. He suggested I talk to his brother Elliott—"Just as good a story-teller," he said—who would be in the day we were dropping by. Not having heard Burr in action, I can't make the comparison. We did enjoy the next hour, though.

Rural, rustic, homespun—the Morse brothers sure measure up as classic "Cracker-Barrel" philosophers. They may not have a lot of time to give, but take what little you can. Elliot sat down with us to chat.

Elliott greeted us in the cross-country ski warming room. (Ski trails are another Morse enterprise.) It was July and we were in no need of warming, but sat down to a great view of the mountains and meadows to the south. Elliott began with a historical introduction to his family, who got their American start in Calais, a few miles to the north. (Pronunciation time-out: "Calais" is pronounced CAL-us. . . . Get over it. Elsewhere in the state, "Berlin is pronounced BUR-lin; "Barre," BEAR-ee; "Leicester," LES-ter; and "Charlotte," shar-LOTT. . . . I said, get over it.)

Anyway, Elliott's great-great-great-great grandfather framed Calais's Old West Church in 1823. "It's exactly as it was then," says Elliott. "It's never had electricity, never had water or bathrooms. And we hope that never will change." He plunged directly into his Old West Church story.

"In 1843, there was this group across the country called Millerites, led by William Miller, who came from the New York shore of Lake Champlain." Disciples of Miller, a former U.S. Army captain and unordained minister, claimed to have discovered when Jesus Christ would return to earth, as stated in the Bible. "His mathematics told him the world would cease to exist on New Year's Eve, 1843," continues Elliott. Millerites were quite widespread across the country, and there was a large group in Calais.

"So that summer, of course, they didn't bother to put up any hay or food for the winter, because they thought they wouldn't need anything. In fact, a few gave away their farms, including their horses and cows. And on New Year's Eve, 1843, they went to the Old West Church, dressed in white Ascension robes. They put a grandfather's clock in front of the altar, and they waited. It was so crowded that some couldn't get in and just looked through the windows. They thought at the stroke of midnight it would all be over. . . . But it wasn't.

"So they waited a few minutes, and then quite dejectedly walked away—because of course they had no horses. And then the Reverend said: 'Well, I guess I made a small mistake.' So he set a date for the following year; and when the same thing happened, that was the end of it. Now, some of these people moved in with relatives. Others found shacks to live in, and that's where they ended their days.

"Well, they didn't string up Reverend Miller, but that religion disappeared, only to evolve into today's Seventh Day Adventists."

Elliott moves right along. "Then, there's the story of the human hibernation. It was a way people in my great-grandfather's day discovered to freeze older people for the winter—because there wasn't enough food for them—and then thaw them in April so they could help with the planting, as well as the fall harvest. . . ."

Sorry. Out of space. For that story, you're going to have to wait for the next edition of *Vermont . . . Who Knew*—or hear it from Elliott himself.

Morse Farm is 2.7 miles northeast of the State Capitol, on Main Street beyond the rotary and just past Center Road on the right. Calais is 10 miles north of Montpelier on Route 12. The Old West Church is in Calais on Old West Church Road, .8 mile south of its intersection with Kent Hill Rd; www.morsefarm.com.

YOUTUBE VIDEO:
"Feeding the Goat at Morse Farm" (:25)
(Actually, the goat takes matters into its own, er, teeth.) 🍁

MARIA VON TRAPP—A LIFETIME OF SERVICE

Stowe

credit: By Royalbroil (CC BY-SA 4.0)

Maria's brother Johannes, who runs the Von Trapp Lodge, spent more than two years in New Guinea with his missionary sister, where he not only learned the language, but built a church, a school, and Maria's house.

Maria was the last survivor of the seven original Von Trapp children. Three half-siblings from her father's second marriage, Rosemarie (born 1928 or 1929), Eleonore (born 1931) and Johannes (born 1939) are still alive but were not featured in "The Sound of Music."

The following profile was written before Maria Franziska von Trapp died at the age of 99 in February, 2014, at her home near the Von Trapp Lodge in Stowe and is adapted from a version that was to appear in the second edition of an earlier book. At her side when she died was her son, Kikuli Mwanukuzi, whom she adopted and raised during her 30 years as a missionary in Papua, New Guinea. Kikuli moved to Galena, IL In 2015 and is teaching high school math at Tri-State Christian School. "I was glad to be there for Maria," he said.

She is not eager to talk about herself. "Read the book," she says, referring to sister Agathe's *Memories Before and After the Sound of Music.* I protest that I have ordered it, but that it is Maria's story I want to hear.

I have come to visit just hours after calling to discuss my old friend Kins Collins' recollections of recorder lessons he took from her at the Trapp Family Lodge decades ago. That was my entrée, but it didn't seem to be working. "There were hundreds of students. I don't remember him," says Maria, reading my e-mail exchanges with Kins. "And he says these were *private* lessons. I don't think I ever gave private lessons." Ah, well. Nobody's fault. It's been fifty years. Memories dissipate.

Maria is a vigorous ninety-six, with a white, waist-length ponytail and still as involved with music as she was more than three-quarters of a century ago. The music stand in the living room of her chalet a mile or so from the lavish grounds of the lodge contains scores for both recorder and accordion. "I can play chords on the accordion, but just the melody on the recorder," she says.

A week after our conversation, Agathe's book arrived. Here is part of what I learned: The Trapp Family Singers, who gave concerts in thirty countries from 1936 to 1956, moved from Austria to the United States in 1938, just before the outbreak of World War II. Their repertoire consisted of sacred music, folk songs, and sixteenth- and seventeenth-century madrigals, sung in English, Italian, and German. Guests who visit the lodge expect Trapp family descendants to break into "Edelweiss" or "Do-Re-Mi" at the drop of an alpenhorn. Few realize that Richard Rodgers and Oscar Hammerstein created this and the other songs for *The Sound of Music* years after the Trapp Family Singers had stopped singing professionally. The distortion of facts structured to accommodate a plot written around these songs brought worldwide acclaim to the family, for reasons that both distressed and bewildered them.

For the most part, though, they are reconciled to the fact that both movie and play have contributed greatly to their lasting fame.

This summary—terse but accurate—convinces Maria that I have done my homework, and we speak again.

She talks a bit about her thirty-two years as a lay missionary in Papua, New Guinea. "I taught singing, did medical work . . . whatever was needed." Sister Rosemarie and brother Johannes (who now runs the lodge) went with her as well. "Johannes stayed for the first two and one-half years and learned the language perfectly. He built a school, a church, and a house for me. Rosemarie taught down there for four years. When we came home for a break, which I had to do occasionally just to get away from the tropics, she stayed home and I returned. She now conducts sing-alongs for guests at the lodge."

Others were no less dedicated. Rupert was a family doctor in Vermont. Werner ran a dairy farm in Waitsfield before his retirement some years ago. (Both enlisted in the Tenth Mountain Division as ski troopers in World War II and fought the Germans in Italy.) Agathe founded a kindergarten in Maryland, which she ran for thirty-seven years. Hedwig, whose severe asthma forced her to live in Hawaii's more forgiving climate, taught youngsters there for several years.

When Maria returned from New Guinea in 1988 at age seventy-four, she brought with her a twenty-six-year-old Tanzanian, Kikuli Mwanukuzi, whom she later adopted. Kikuli, a math tutor at Johnson State College, has aspirations of being governor of Vermont one day. I ask if he has his citizenship. "Not yet," he says, "but it won't be long. If Schwarzenegger can do it, why can't I?"

Directions: To reach the Trapp Family Lodge, take Route 100 north to the outskirts of Stowe. Take a left on Moscow Road and follow the signs to 100 Trapp Hill Road. For more information visit www.trappfamily.com, or call (800) 826-7000.

YouTube Video:
"So Long, farewell: Maria von Trapp dies at 99" (2:53)
(A tribute by Channel 4) ❦

HIGH SCHOOL DROPOUT TRANSFORMS COLLEGE EDUCATION

Strafford

A goodly number of this country's 105 land grant colleges and universities—Iowa State, Cornell University, the University of Vermont, and Washington State University among them—have a Morrill Hall on campus. Largely this is because if it weren't for Senator Justin Smith Morrill, those institutions would not exist. In 1862 President Abraham Lincoln signed the Morrill Land-Grant Colleges Act, written and fought for by Senator Morrill for the previous seven years. This act allocated funds from the sales of public lands to support new colleges that taught agriculture, engineering, business, and home economics. It opened the door for poor and minority students to pursue a college education.

Justin Morrill grew up in Strafford, Vermont, and eagerly looked forward to attending college, but his family was too poor to send him. He left school for good at age fifteen. His interest in architecture, horticulture, and politics, though, was intense enough for him to become learned in all three. After seventeen years as a merchant and seven as a farmer, Morrill was elected to the Congress, and eventually the U.S. Senate, serving in one body or another for nearly fifty years. Today more than 25 million graduates have Senator Morrill to thank for their college education.

The Gothic Revival homestead and farm complex in Strafford was designed by Justin Morrill and built for him in 1848. The house is furnished with original and family pieces. Interpretive exhibits are located in several of the barns and outbuildings.

Directions: From Route 132 in South Strafford, take the Justin Smith Morrill Highway and go 2 miles to the Strafford Village. The homestead is located on the right-hand side of the road on the north end of the village. The homestead is open from Memorial Day to Columbus Day, Saturday and Sunday 11:00 a.m. to 5:00 p.m. For more information visit www.morrillhomestead.org. ❦

"HEY NORMAN, YOU'VE LOST YOUR NECK"

Thetford

In 1986, after publishing her first book of poetry, Grace Paley helped form a women's committee for International PEN, the writers' group advocating freedom of expression. When the committee questioned that only 16 of 117 panelists at PEN's 48th congress were women, then president and novelist Norman Mailer responded that the speakers had to be of "real distinction." (Panelist Susan Sontag, one of the 16 who had not joined the protest, said instead: "Literature is not an equal opportunity employer.")

"I used to feel I could talk to [Mailer], since both of us came from the Bronx," Paley recalled in a *Vermont Woman* interview in 2007. "So I said once, 'Norman, don't talk that way. It's very upsetting to women.' And he said, 'They're just getting older and uglier, that's all.' That was the end of my trying, So now when I see him at things . . . and *he's* older, I think to myself: *Hey Norman, you've lost your neck.*"

Grace Paley moved to Thetford in 1972 after marrying her second husband, poet and activist Robert Nichols. "I feel lucky to be here," she said about living in Vermont, "but I was lucky to live in New York City, too. Both places are different and also exciting to me. I wouldn't be who I am if I hadn't had both."

Paley's short fiction includes three story collections: *The Little Disturbances of Man, Enormous Changes at the Last Minute,* and *Later the Same Day.* Philip Roth (whose own short-story collection, like Paley's, was published in 1959) wrote about "Little Disturbances" that Paley had "an understanding of loneliness, lust, selfishness and fatigue that is splendidly comic and unladylike." Her gift of "pitch-perfect dialogue" was universally acclaimed.

The Collected Stories, a reissue of her three previous works, was a 1994 National Book Award Finalist for Fiction. Paley was Poet Laureate of Vermont from 2003-2007.

Grace Paley died at her Thetford home of breast cancer in August, 2007.

YOUTUBE VIDEOS:
"Grace Paley Documentary by Sonya Friedman" (3:17)
(Excerpts citing her activism—as important to her as writing)

"Grace Paley and the 'Disturbances of Man' Walking Tour" (3:26)
(Greenwich Village tour of scenes from the book and Paley's
neighborhood) ❧

RIP, BOVINITY DIVINITY

Waterbury

**Coconut Cream Pie Low-Fat Ice Cream, Honey Apple
Raisin Chocolate Cookie, KaBerry KABOOM!, Makin'
Whoopee Pie, Ooey Gooey Cake Frozen Yogurt, Peanuts!
Popcorn! Peppermint Schtick . . . Had enough?**

Up an imposing hill and beyond a much less imposing parking
lot, a white picket fence surrounds a grove of beech trees. In these
peaceful confines you'll find Ben & Jerry's Flavor Graveyard, a

repository for ill-named or ill-conceived ice cream concoctions that have failed the test of consumer approval. I was looking for a headstone that commemorated a real doozy, perhaps a Garlic Lamb Fat Fudge Swirl or a Carrot Tomato Vegan Delight. Instead I spy a dead flavor I would have graded a definite keeper: Maine Blueberry Ice Cream. What could have happened? Was it too down home? Too ordinary? No. Too seasonal. From the inscription I learn that when summer faded, this flavor's sales did as well.

But here's an envelope pusher even I could have predicted: Tennessee Mud had Loser stamped on its one-pint carton from at least two directions. Bourbon lovers looking for a taste treat reminding them of a favored beverage—and perhaps a wee buzz?—turned up their noses. Parents fearing residual traces of alcohol likely were driven to the safer scoops of Howard Johnson's 31 Flavors, or a local ice creamery. (The ingredients were said to include a taste of "Jack Daniel's Old No. 7 Tennessee Sour Mash Whiskey," a contention the B&J public relations department, after several phone calls, would neither confirm nor deny.) The epitaph says it all:

THE BOTTLE IS EMPTY,
THE CUP AND THE GLASS.
MUD WITH JACK DANIEL'S
WAS NOT MEANT TO LAST.
1988–1989

Discovering other flavors that deserved capital punishment, you may be as glad as I was to hear that Economic Crunch, Honey I'm Home, and Bovinity Divinity have gotten their just desserts.

The Flavor Graveyard is on the grounds of Ben & Jerry's Waterbury factory, the company's flagship manufacturing plant. Ben & Jerry's happens to be one of the nation's best companies in terms of social responsibility, their mission reading, in part: "Initiating ways to improve the quality of life locally, nationally, and internationally." Even after being absorbed by corporate giant Unilever, B&J has been able to retain and act on its long-held progressive values. Tours of the Waterbury factory are conducted seven days a week year-round, except for Thanksgiving, Christmas, and New Year's Day. Hours vary by season. For more information visit www.benjerry.com/scoop_shops/factory_tour or call (802) 882-1240, extension 2285.

YouTube Video:
"A Tour of the Ben & Jerry's Factory" (5:51) 🍁

Spiderweb Man

Williamstown

Will Knight died at his beloved Spider Web Farm in June, 2017. Spider-web fans need not worry, though. Just one year almost to the day later, Will, Jr. and widow Terry had the farm up and running again. There's a new spider barn that replaces the one destroyed by fire. Not only that; Terry and young Will are perfecting their story-telling

skills as they similarly develop expertise raising spiders and running the farm. Here's Spider Web Farm founder Will at work on a day I visited him some years ago.

"I have a grandson," says Will Knight, "a graduate of Rensselaer. Had a job before he even got out of college. He's a crackerjack on the computer."

"'Gramps,' he says to me one day—he was like fifteen or sixteen—'you oughta get on that Internet.'

"I said, 'You know, you're the second guy to tell me that.'" Will pauses for effect. "'I told the first guy *I* was the original website.'"

You can almost hear the rim shot. Will's timing and delivery are superb, as if he's told this story a thousand times, which of course he has. "So my grandson says, 'I'll put you right on it, Gramps.' And the next thing you know, I had a new kind of web site."

We're at Knight's Spider Web Farm, said to be the only one of its kind in the world. Forty years ago, Will moved to Vermont from Brooklyn with his wife and four children. A professional real estate appraiser, he got a job with the state transportation department while Interstate 91 was being built, negotiating with families who were displaced by the construction. "We took a lot of houses up there," he says. "Fifty-six in Saint Johnsbury alone."

But when the highway was finished Will was out of a job. He was a good woodworker, though, and built miniature cabinets to sell at craft shows around the state. But he soon tired of the constant travel, and few people wanted to come to him.

"One day my wife collected a spiderweb on a piece of wood and painted a flower on it," he recalls. "A fellow came in, looked around, and asked if we had any plain webs. He said, 'If you did, I think you'd have a market.'

"Then for some reason, I forget why, I got invited to Faneuil Hall, in Boston—a huge market. I took about 500 webs down there, and in a week we sold about 350. So I came back and built more web frames. See that shed out there? There's space in it for about 300 webs. I can get 275 more in the garage, and another 240 in those metal frames next to it."

Will has perfected his business over the years by listening to ideas from friends. And each improvement has its own story.

"One day back then a guy came in, a friend of my wife's from community college and a business planner in the Salmon administration [Vermont governor Tom Salmon, 1973–1977]. Bert was his name. He came in and looked at one of my webs and said, 'What are you going to do with this?'

"I say, 'It hangs on the wall, Bert. It's a plaque. What you think of it?'

"'Pretty,' he says. Then a minute later he says, 'Look around the room and tell me what you see—everything that hangs there.'

"'Bert,' I say, 'no games! Tell me what I can do to improve things.'

"'Well, I'm telling you,' he says. 'Everything hanging in this room has a frame, *except your plaques.*'

"And then I saw it. This was a way to finish my product! And that's the way these things happen."

Here's Will on pricing:

"A friend of mine in Barre—big-time kitchen developer—told me I wasn't getting enough money for these plaques. He first told me that thirty years ago when I was getting $4.95.

"'Willy, you're making a mistake. You're giving them away. What the hell is $4.95,' he says. 'You gotta sell twenty to make $100. Why don't you ask $50, and then you'll only have to sell two!'

"I say, 'Claude, who the hell is going to pay $50 for a plaque?'

"'You'll see,' he said. And he was right. A man came in a month later with his wife. I had one hanging up here—a big one—and I had written on it with white correction fluid, as a joke: "Goodbye, Wilbur." [For those who haven't read *Charlotte's Web*, Wilbur is the pig afraid of ending up on the dinner table.] His wife was looking around outside, and he came over to my counter with the plaque. "I'll take this one," he said.

"I said, 'Sorry, That's not for sale.'

"'I don't think you heard me,' he said. 'I'll take it.'

"So I walked around the counter and got a big bag; I put the plaque in the bag with one of my flyers and said: 'Now is that going to be cash or credit?'

"He says, 'Cash.' He never asked me how much it was.

So I said, 'Okay, that'll be one hundred plus tax. He never said a word!

"He says to his wife, 'Agnes,' he says, 'I got one for your class.' It turns out she's a teacher and he's a superintendent of schools from wherever the hell they came from, and she does a whole unit on *Charlotte's Web*. I felt bad. For a hundred bucks. But not *my* hundred bucks! Well, it is now."

Directions: Take exit 5 on I-89 toward Williamstown and stay on Route 14 going south through the village. Turn right onto Spider Web Farm Road, the naming of which is another good story. For more information visit www.spiderwebfarm.com or call (802) 433-5568. ❦

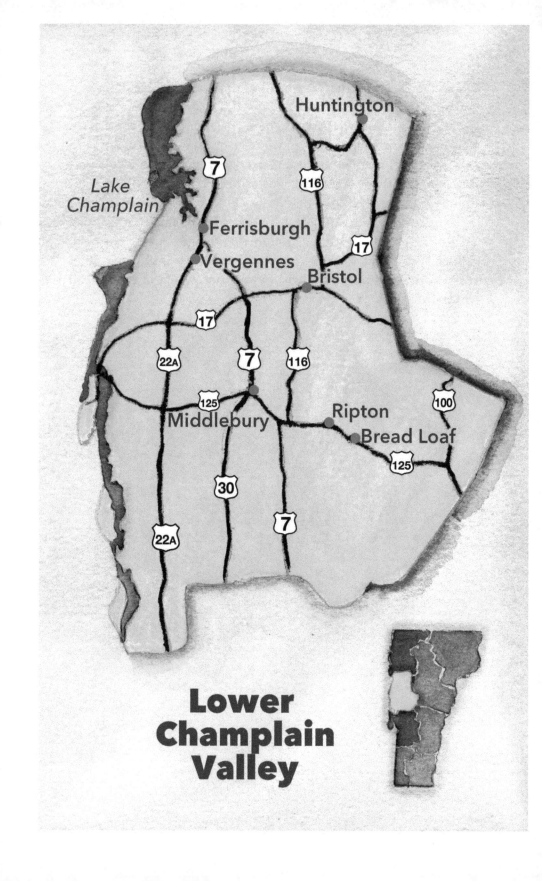

Lower
Champlain
Valley

7

LOWER CHAMPLAIN VALLEY

A good chunk of the Lake Champlain Maritime Museum's exhibits are hidden—some 350 feet or more beneath the lake's surface. So how do interested parties see them? Until 2004 only certified scuba divers had access. That was the year that museum technicians discovered a way to equip their remotely operated vehicles (ROVs) with video equipment that could project live underwater pictures directly to visitors in tour boats. What treasures await!

Once in a while a personal story comes along that just feels good to tell. For more than fifteen years, Pat Palmer of Bristol has conducted one of the most unique and self-contained trash collection systems ever devised. His two associates, Jake and Jerry, are full-fledged partners, and the entire operation would go to seed without them. What a team!

Decades before the Civil War, an "underground railroad" of men and women helped runaway slaves who had escaped their lives of desperation but had nowhere to go. Some "agents" for the fugitives hid them temporarily until a family up north was found to offer employment and education. The Robinsons, in Ferrisburgh, were such a family. The Rokeby Museum tells their story, and those of the dozens of men and women who lived with them until they were prepared for new lives of freedom in Vermont or elsewhere.

ROBERT F. WILSON

VERMONT'S ONE-OF-A-KIND GARBAGE PICK-UP SERVICE

Bristol

For thirty years, Bristol's road crew had picked up the town's garbage every week. But when a new administrator came to town, he decided the road crew should *remain* on the road, and that garbage pick-up should be privatized. Patrick Palmer's bid was the lowest, so he was awarded the contract. Pat didn't have a truck, but he did have a wagon and a team of horses. He lived in New Haven just one town away and figured that a job covering roughly 300 homes and businesses seemed manageable. And it was, for the next nine years. Then two years ago a Bristol official said the town could not afford Pat anymore.

"They wouldn't give me a deal to dump the trash in their landfill, which is still open," says Pat. So he got in touch with Scott Olson, a division manager for Casella Waste Systems, which services the Middlebury area. "I asked him if Casella wanted to buy my business. Instead he asked me what *I* wanted to do. I said I liked the job and wanted to keep doing it."

Upshot: Pat and Scott Olson worked out an arrangement whereby every Friday instead of going to the Bristol landfill, Pat transferred both trash and recycled materials onto one of Casella's rear loaders at a drop-off point in town. A couple of years ago when Casella raised Its prices, Pat changed "distributors" again. The Gauther Trucking Company also accepts the recycling pre-separated, as opposed to Pat separating paper from bottles from cans, and so on, himself.

So this becomes an illustration not only of Vermont ingenuity at its best, but a rare example of a corporation serving both community and entrepreneur, at the expense of primacy to the bottom line.

To continue in a parallel "green" vein, here is how Pat has arranged his business (and this Is with no tractors, only horses): On his farm he raises hay, with the help of his horses, Jake and Jerry, for all planting, cultivating, and harvesting, meaning of course that he uses no gas or oil. He feeds the hay to his horses, which not only eat well but supply the manure (and the horsepower to spread it), to in turn help ensure a good crop. The horses' good health allows them to work with Pat to collect the community's trash and recyclables over time, which in turn helps to complete another cycle—that of man's attempt to better live in harmony with nature, which indeed is what this particular man is doing.

Now to the intrigue that, if one looks for it, is part of just about any vocation. Pat has his customers buy yellow stickers at Martin's Hardware that they put on each bag for collection. (The recycling is free.) Sometimes a crafty customer will "forget" to put on a sticker. Sometimes a less-than-honest customer will steal a sticker from another bag. Sometimes a customer will wrap half a sticker around the plastic string at the top of some bags, on the grounds that it will be appear to be a whole sticker. Pat, ever vigilant, knows all the tricks. Those unstickered or semi-stickered bags remain uncollected, until the misdemeanors are rectified.

Not that Pat or his horses are off-duty every day but Friday. He recently signed on to add Middlebury to his schedule and is thinking he may need a three-horse wagon to accommodate it There is also sap to be collected in the spring, sleigh rides in the winter, carriage rides for weddings, wagon rides for special events, and wood to be gathered. "I also do some logging for people and occasionally pull a moose out of the national forest in season." He's had the team he uses now for seven years. As a general rule they have a working life of up to fifteen years.

So do the horses get any leisure time?

"Oh yeah," says Pat. "Just as much as I do."

If you're in Bristol on a Friday or Tuesday in Middlebury (where he now needs a three-horse rig)—or any other day Pat happens to be out and about—make it a point to wave to him. You could say hi to Jake and Jerry, too. Better yet, bring along a carrot or two. It'll be Ok with Pat.

YouTube Video:
"Horse-drawn Trash Service Delights Vermont Towns" (1:37) ❧

A MUSEUM OF TREASURES, BOTH SEEN AND UNSEEN

Ferrisburgh

The twelve-bolt helmet was used by deep-sea divers from the 1830s to the 1970s, until it was replaced by SCUBA equipment. Try one on at the Lake Champlain Maritime Museum!

Art Cohn, executive director emeritus and cofounder of the Lake Champlain Maritime Museum, defines the museum's mission as one "preserving and sharing the history and archaeology of the region, and the study and management of underwater cultural resources." According to Cohn, the exhibit that most thoroughly embodies this mission, as well as the museum's ongoing work, is the one featuring the canal schooner *General Butler*.

"It's a perfect example of underwater resource management," says Cohn. "The 88-foot wooden remains of a canal boat located in Burlington harbor . . . has been a major focus of our research. True heroism was involved in the rescue of the shipwrecked people. It has the blue-collar, day-to-day commerce these boats represented. It has the canal era, a major focus of our study. And it's got underwater resource management all over it." A full-sized replica displayed in the museum is modeled from detailed archaeological measurements.

Sunk in a violent storm in December 1876, the *General Butler* was discovered by divers in 1980. Here is its story, taken from contemporary eyewitness and press accounts: William Montgomery was captaining the *General Butler* (named after a Massachusetts lawyer and Civil War hero) one Saturday in December when heavy gales drove the vessel toward the Burlington breakwater. *General Butler* was carrying a load of Isle La Motte marble for delivery to the Burlington Marble Works. Also on board were a deckhand, Montgomery's teenage daughter Cora and her schoolgirl friend, and a quarry operator from Isle La Motte.

The power of the storm was too much for the steering mechanism of the aging schooner, and just off the breakwater, the vessel began to drift southward. The deckhand threw over the storm anchor in a vain attempt to keep the vessel from crashing into the breakwater's stone-filled cribs. Meanwhile, Captain Montgomery chained a spare tiller bar onto the ship's steering gear. He then ordered the anchor line severed with an axe and attempted to round the southern end of the breakwater, but despite his efforts, a short distance from the southern lighthouse, *General Butler* instead smashed into the breakwater.

The passengers and crew were able to leap free of the wreckage onto the breakwater. The captain was last to leave the ship and barely made it to safety after jumping at the crest of a large wave. The *General Butler* sank immediately, its stone cargo propelling it downward. Stranded on the open breakwater, whipped by fierce winds and driving snow, the canal boat's refugees might have died were it not for James Wakefield and his son, Jack. The two untied a small government lighthouse boat and rowed out to the break-water. Captain Montgomery lifted his daughter and her friend into James Wakefield's arms and then clambered aboard himself after the deckhand and the quarry operator had jumped into the bobbing rowboat.

Although the masts, rigging, and some other equipment were recovered, the hull of the *General Butler* was not. Today, it rests in 40 feet of water at the south end of Burlington's breakwater. You'll be able to imagine for yourself what it was like aboard an 1862-class canal boat by climbing the gangplank of the schooner *Lois McClure*, in residence at the museum's Basin Harbor facility during the summer and used as a periodic teaching tool in Vermont and New York schools and communities.

This is a simple sample of the surprises that await a curious visitor to the Lake Champlain Maritime Museum. Spend some time on its website (www.cmm.org) to familiarize yourself with the range of available activities and outreach programs (kindergarten through graduate school), and the opportunity to observe rowing, boat-building, metalworking and blacksmithing in workshops. Heads-up: A tour led by director of collections and exhibits Eloise Beil will be particularly rewarding, thanks both to her passion and her encyclopedic knowledge of the museum's vast range of exhibits and activities.

Directions: Because several different routes are involved depending on your city of origin, separate directions from Burlington, Boston, Montreal and New York are printed on the museum website. The following directions are for those of you from Vermont and arriving from the south (on Route 7) or east after leaving I-91 (Exit 2 in Brattleboro). Follow U.S. Route 4 to Route 22A and drive north 40 miles to Vergennes. Turn left on Panton Road, and go 1 mile. Then turn right on Basin Harbor Road, and go 6 miles to the museum on right, at 4472 Basin Harbor Road. The museum is open late May through late October, 10:00 a.m. to 5:00 p.m. daily. To get an idea of the host of activities the maritime museum provides, inquire about visiting the *Lois McClure*, or find out general information, visit www.lcmm.org, or call (802) 475-2022.

YOUTUBE VIDEOS:
"Sailing Canal Boat General Butler" (2:00)
(Viewing her today in her underwater home)

"Building the Jimmy D" (3:18
(Ever see a longboat built in three minutes?) ❦

VERMONT'S UNDERGROUND RAILROAD

Ferrisburgh

On a ninety-acre site on U.S. Route 7 in Ferrisburgh is the Rokeby Museum, a National Historic Landmark judged to be the best documented stop on the Underground Railway. In the decades leading up to the Civil War, Rowland T. Robinson and his wife, Rachel, harbored dozens of fugitive slaves at their farm and provided them with the employment and education that would prepare them to start new lives in the North.

The Robinsons were devout Quakers who believed that slavery was a sin to be opposed by every acceptable means. Their beliefs were buttressed by living In a state that had banned slavery In 1777, when It was a sovereign nation—and 88 years before the 13th Amendment to the Constitution became law. The thousands of letters in the family's collection reveal exactly what the escaped slaves went through as they risked severe punishment or worse to escape their lives of desperation. Some of these letters offer illuminating case studies of specific individuals, lending identities to their customary anonymity.

What one takes from an experience at Rokeby Museum is the realization that for those fugitive slaves who made it as far as Vermont, there would be no more hiding for fear of capture. Somewhat farther south—in a slave border state like Maryland, for example, or a free border state like Pennsylvania—runaway slaves were generally caught. They had to travel with utmost caution until they reached Massachusetts, at least. Sometimes antislavery agents in states south of Vermont performed a service similar to that of recruiters and personnel counselors today, attempting to match a prospective employee's skills and accomplishments with an employer's perceived needs. The following letter excerpts, for example, were compiled by Rokeby Museum director Jane Williamson as part of a winter 2001 *Vermont History* article.

One correspondent was Oliver Johnson, a Vermonter and newspaper editor who helped a number of fugitives from states to the south. In 1837 Johnson wrote Rowland Robinson from Jenner

Township in Pennsylvania. The runaway he had found, Simon, was wanted for a sizable reward.

"When he came here, he was destitute of clothing, and unable to proceed," wrote Johnson. "William C. Griffith, the son of a friend, who has often rendered assistance to runaways, kindly offered to keep him until spring. . . . It is not considered safe for him to remain here after winter has gone by, as search will no doubt be made for him.

"He is 28 years old," Johnson continued, "and appeared to me to be an honest, likely man. . . . I was so well pleased with his appearance that I could not help thinking he would be a good man for you to hire. Mr. Griffith says that he is very trustworthy, of a kind disposition, and knows how to do almost all kinds of farm work. He is used to teaming and is very good to manage horses. He says that he could beat any man in the neighborhood where he lived at mowing, cradling, or pitching."

New York City Quaker and store owner Joseph Beale said of fugitive Jeremiah Snowden in 1842 that "Brother John Nickolson thinks Jeremiah can be very useful to a farmer needing such a man." And later that it would be "safer for him to be in Massachusetts or Vermont if work is to be had for him. We were unwilling to risk his remaining, although we had abundance of work for him at this busy season."

New York Quaker and antislavery agent Charles Marriott assured Robinson that John Williams "was a good chopper and farmer," and that his wife, Martha, was "useful and well conducted in the house . . . The recent decision of the Supreme Court as to the unconstitutionality of jury trial laws for them has decided us to send them further north either to you or to Canada . . . If they could be taken in by thee, we should think them safer."

Each of the correspondents makes clear to the fugitives that Vermont is a safe haven, and that those few who had considered going as far as Canada had no need to do so. In its day Rokeby was one of the most prosperous farms in the Champlain Valley, and an ideal transitional destination for slaves preparing themselves for lives as free men and women.

On-site are the main house and most of the original outbuildings, plus hiking trails over more than fifty acres of farmland and orchards. The house may be seen by guided tour in groups limited to twelve. Tours last forty-five minutes.

Directions: On U.S. Route 7, 2 miles south of the North Ferrisburgh village center, watch for the historic site marker and front entrance sign on the east side of the road. The museum is open from mid-May to mid-October. House tours are offered three times a day, Thursday through Sunday, but the rest of the farm and museum are open to self-guided tours. For more information visit www.rokeby.org or call (802) 877-3406. ❧

BEST "LITTLE MUSEUM" IN THE STATE

Middlebury

Community museums—community *anything*, it seems—often get a bad rap in favor of larger venues. If you appreciate art and history, though, not giving the Henry Sheldon Museum several hours of your time would be a mistake. Chartered in 1882 as an art museum and archeological and historical society, it offers fine and folk art, period furniture, musical instruments, clocks, toys, as well as primary documentary source material tracing the history of Middlebury and the Mid-Lake Champlain region.

Our guide on a stimulating tour of Judd-Harris House, the museum's main building, was executive director William F. Brooks Jr. Bill Brooks is steeped in folk art knowledge from decades of managing a number of galleries and craft centers in various parts of the state.

Well before Henry Sheldon created his museum—and even before he bought the Judd-Harris House—he boarded there from owners Eben Judd and his son-in-law, Lebbeus Harris. But even on his salary as a railway agent and organist at the Episcopal Church, he was able to collect items that became the core of the Henry Sheldon Museum.

Bill divided his time with us between the museum's permanent exhibits and a retrospective revolving exhibit by Warren Kimble, on display for six months. Area artists who participate often are available for weekly one-hour "Gallery Talks," describing their work and taking questions from museum visitors. Works by the contemporary artists are often on display in the historic period rooms.

(public domain)

Nathaniel Chipman. U.S. Senator from Vermont. (Oil on canvas, circa 1800.Henry Sheldon Museum of History, Middlebury, Vermont

Some of the permanent exhibits are arranged as a house would be at a specific point in time. Kitchen, dining room, bedroom, children's room in, say, a colonial household, all are furnished appropriately, to more easily visualize the particulars of daily living for a given period. Bill also introduced us to collection storage on the third floor, the attic, the basement and the barn by opening closets and cabinets to see other treasures. "I am hoping to include this in a future American folk-art exhibit," he said, running his hands over a six-foot chain, links carved from a single piece of wood.

As for the museum's other three buildings and gardens, the barn was built by Henry Sheldon around 1890 for horses and carriages. The Walter Cerf Gallery was named after an art dealer and philanthropist who taught philosophy at Brooklyn College for 24 years after emigrating from Nazi Europe in the late 1930s. In 1972 he moved to Leicester and began philanthropic activity.

The Stewart-Swift Research Center is the third of the Museum's buildings and was built in 1972 with the support of Jessica Swift. Actually it was courtesy of Charles Swift, Jessica's late second husband and his trolley car investments in the Philippines that she was able to give whatever she wished to whomever she wished. The oldest piece of the archival collection dates from 1357; the newest, from 2010. It includes more than7,000 photographs, 450 maps, 4,000 books and pamphlets, 250 years' worth of newspaper print going back to 1801, and 800 linear feet of manuscripts (family records, diaries, letters, and scrapbooks). Nearly all the photographs are catalogued and span the entire history of photographic media from daguerreotypes to digital images.

With advanced notice, director Bill Brooks offers personalized tours. For directions, hours, and special events, see www.henry-sheldonmuseum.org.

YOUTUBE VIDEOS:
"Fashion & Fantasy at the Edge of the Forest at the Henry Sheldon Museum" (3:58)
(Narrated by Bill Brooks)

"Warren Kimble YouTube Sharing" (7:17)
(The artist describes eclectic works displayed at the Henry Sheldon Museum) ✤

ROBERT FROST—THE BREAD LOAF YEARS

Ripton

Robert Frost spent his Vermont years either in Shaftsbury, in the south, or in Ripton, in the central part of the state. It was in Ripton that Frost developed a forty-year attachment to the prestigious Bread Loaf Writers' Conference, which he founded in 1926.

In 1921 Frost joined the Bread Loaf School of English, started the year before at Middlebury College. The Bread Loaf Mountain campus, vacant from mid-August to the end of the month, struck Frost as an ideal location to convene writers eager to improve their skills, with the help of established professionals who would serve as mentors. He made this idea stick and in 1926 presided over the Bread Loaf Writers' Conference inaugural session.

Until 1962, the year before he died, Frost was there nearly every year, as faculty member, speaker, or fellow. He was so ubiquitous, in fact, that writer and editor Louis Untermeyer referred to Bread Loaf as "the most Frost-bitten place in America." Frost himself had mixed feelings about the direction of the conference, in particular a growing emphasis on matching writers with editors and literary agents. He once called Bread Loaf the Two Weeks' Manuscript Sales Fair.

After the death of his wife in 1938, Frost bought the Homer Noble Farm in Ripton, comprising several hundred acres of fields and forest near the Bread Loaf campus, including a barn and a cabin. He was so smitten with Kathleen Morrison, a staff member at Bread Loaf and the wife of conference director Ted Morrison, that he asked her to marry him later that same year. She refused but became his secretary for the rest of his life, living in the farmhouse with Ted while Frost occupied the cabin. (No information so far as to what that chain of events did to their respective relationships.) Frost lived there summers until he died in 1963.

Two miles east of Ripton is the Robert Frost Wayside Area, where the Robert Frost Interpretive Trail begins. This idyllic, 3/4-mile tribute to the poet includes seven of his poems mounted on plaques, at intervals on sets dressed by a rushing brook visible beyond the trees or a clearing exposing a Green Mountains backdrop.

Directions: The Robert Frost Memorial Drive, a 14-mile route through woods, farmlands, and mountains, starts at the junction of U.S. Route 7 and Route 125, and 2 miles east of Ripton, on Route 125, is the Robert Frost Wayside Area, where the Robert Frost Interpretive Trail begins. For more information about the Bread Loaf Writers' Conference, visit www.middlebury.edu/academics/blwc.

YOUTUBE VIDEOS:
"Robert Frost Trail" (1:44)
(Dizziness Alert!)

"Bread Loaf Inn Remembered-May 2015" (19:50)
(Historical summary and walking tour) ❧

VERMONT'S SHEEP HEYDAY

In Vermont's sheep heyday Addison County counted 373 sheep
per square mile. This Vermont County raised more sheep and
produced more wool, in proportion to its size and population,
than any other county in the United States. The Vermont sheep
industry allowed a burgeoning wool-processing industry to arise
here as well. Carding mills, which first appeared in Vermont in
the 1790s, combed raw wool to prepare it for spinning. Fulling
mills washed and sized the woof fiber, or woolen cloth. In 1829
Vermont had twenty-nine carding mills and fifty-eight fulling
mills. By 1820 there were four times as many of these mills
throughout the state.

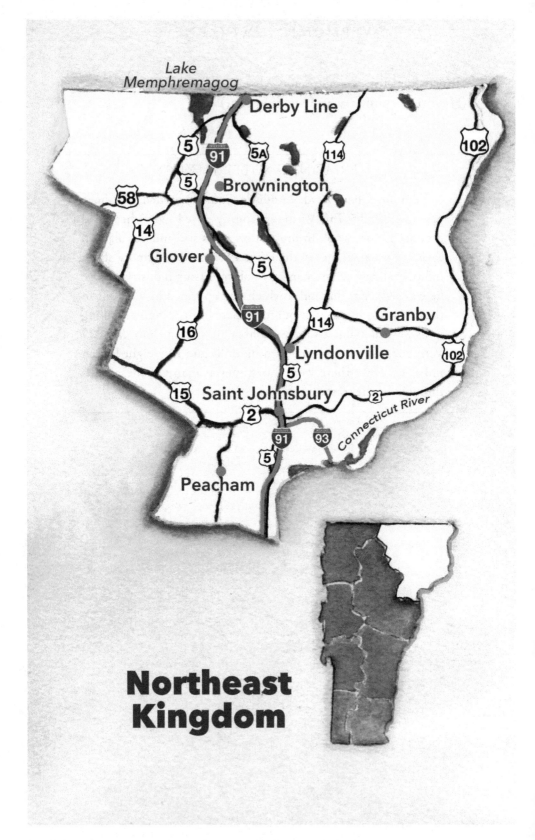

Lake
Memphremagog

Derby Line

5 · 91 · 5A · 114 · 102

5 · Brownington

58

14

Glover · 5

16 · 91 · 114 · Granby · 102

Lyndonville

5

15 · Saint Johnsbury · 2

2 · 91 · 93 · Connecticut River

5

Peacham

**Northeast
Kingdom**

8

NORTHEAST KINGDOM

The folks at Saint Johnsbury's Fairbanks Museum will roll their eyes when visitors focus on the upper-floor "bug art." There's much else to entrance the most jaded visitor, after all: a planetarium; a meteorological center, with a dozen or more weather forecasts beamed over Vermont Public Radio daily; and 75,000 mounted reptiles, mammals, fish, and birds, including 131 species of hummingbirds, the largest such collection in North America, we're told. But there's no more curiosity-friendly exhibit than the nine works of dead butterflies and beetles arranged to depict historical events. Yes, 13,555 of these poor devils gave their lives to create a display of Old Glory honoring the Articles of Confederation. We're told that the daughter of artist (in quotes?) John Hampson called museums all over the country to plead for bug-art perpetuity before the Fairbanks agreed. There's a relief.

And that's not the only museum In the Northeast Kingdom—we have two more to tell you about. They're quite different from each other, as well. Their names alone will be enough for you to want to hear more: The Bread and Puppet Theater Is a performance center as well as a museum. The Museum of Everyday Things gets down to the basics. We're not talking about the arcane, the extinct, the endangered, or the unusual. Its first four exhibits were the match, the pencil, the safety pin and the tooth brush. Read on; you'll be surprised.

THE FORKED STICK SOCIETY

Good dowsers are known for their ability to find sources of underground water. The best dowsers are known for their ability to find lost items, track criminals, locate missing persons, and seek guidance of a more spiritual nature. Since its founding in 1958, in Danville, Vermont, the focus of the American Society of Dowsers has expanded from simply seeking water to include many uses and practices of dowsing. (For more information visit the American Society of Dowser's Web site at www.dowsers.org.)

—Chris Burns
The Vermont Encyclopedia

THE AUDIENCE IS IN VERMONT; THE PERFORMERS ARE IN CANADA

Derby Line

That would be the Haskell Opera House, with one minor qualification: As you will see by the blue borderline when you visit, there actually are a few seats on the Canadian side. For fourteen seasons, QNEK (Quebec Northeast Kingdom) Productions has staged lively and varied musicals, revues, comedies, children's shows, and plays, all acted by its resident theater company.

Downstairs is the Haskell Free Library. Proceeds from the opera house assure that it is *really* free. "No rentals; no membership fees," says librarian Mary Roy. "We do have fines [for overdue books], though. A whopping two cents a day." (The librarians accept either U.S. or Canadian currency, on the grounds that things will pretty much even out at the end of the month.) By the way, a look at the blue borderline on the library reading room floor will quickly tell you why this building is sometimes called "the only U.S. library with no books; the only Canadian theater with no stage."

Did you guess that the line on the floor is an international boundary? Does the arrow help? (That's why we're here.)

Modeled after the now defunct Boston Opera House, the neo-classical building was built to straddle the international border between Derby Line and what is now Stanstead, Quebec. American sawmill owner Carlos Haskell and his Canadian wife, Martha Stewart Haskell, wanted it to be used by people in both countries.

Directions: Take exit 29 on Interstate 91; turn left over the bridge, go down the hill, and stop at the largest brick building in town, visible on the right, at 93 Caswell Avenue. The library is open year-round, Tuesday, Wednesday, and Friday, 10:00 a.m.–5:00 p.m., and Thursday, 10:00 a.m.–8:00 p.m. For more information visit www.haskellopera.org, or call the library at (802) 873-3022.

The opera house's season runs from April to October. For concert tickets or information, call QNEK productions at (802) 334-2216 or visit www.qnek.com.

N.B.:If you plan to cross the Derby "line," the border into Canada, and are sixteen or over, you'll need your birth certificate and a photo ID—or a passport.

YouTube Video
"For These Border Towns, the Only Wall Is a Row of Potted Plants" (4:46)
(But changes are evident since 9/11—ABC News) ❦

Library Lover?

Vermont Is filled with unique libraries, a complete list of which, plus addresses and contact Information, can be found on the web under "Vermont Public Libraries."

In Canaan, the state's most northeastern town, the 170-year-old library was the next-to-last stagecoach stop on a route from Franklin, NH to Montreal, Canada. It was placed on the National Register of Historic Places In 1890.

Farther south Is the Windsor Public Library, which lends not only books but non-genetically-modified seeds suited to the local climate. Patrons can borrow whole packets and return them full after harvesting their crops. Gardening and seed-saving information is also available.

The Brooks Memorial Library, even farther south In Brattleboro, houses an extensive art collection, an interesting collection of artifacts, and a self-guided fine-arts walking tour downtown.

THE BREAD AND PUPPET THEATER

Glover

Home for Bread and Puppet's thousands of papier mâché masks, puppets, and props are two levels of a recently renovated 140-year-old hay barn, which also houses a bookshop.

Such a cute name, is your first thought if you don't know better. But this is not your mama's down-home country theater, even if it is set in the countryside a couple of miles outside the village of Glover. True, the bread and the puppets are real enough. For the past half-century loaves of crusty sourdough bread have been baked and distributed with aioli (mayonnaise-garlic sauce) after each performance by director/founder Peter Schumann. "Theater is like bread," Schumann has said. "A necessity."

But Schumann, a German-born performance artist and sculptor, has not assembled his ensemble and the works they present for entertainment alone. He is here to inform, to protest—to provoke thought and action. This is pure political theater. Schumann's brand was born in 1963 during the Vietnam War, to give voice to frustrated protesters powerless to stop the fighting. It moved from New York to Vermont in 1970. Since then the troupe has performed all over the United States and in Europe, Latin America, and Asia.

The B&P ensemble at work one sunny Sunday August afternoon.

I have read that Peter Schumann is viewed by some as a hero, and by others as an anarchist, a fact which I mention to Linda Elbow, the group's tour and business manager.

"What's the matter with being an anarchist?" says Linda. I'm on her side. This is what created both the United States and, at about the same time, the sovereign nation of Vermont. We agree that to some it is a loaded word, even the equivalent of *traitor*.

"Some people don't like to watch us," says Linda. "Where were we last week? . . . Oh, Glover Day! Every year we put on a performance for Glover Day, a show called *Runaway Pond,* commemorating a tragedy that happened here in 1810. Its bicentennial was celebrated a few years back. There had been a drought that year and not enough water was available to turn the wheel at the mill. Some local fellows went down to a nearby pond to dig a ditch that would let water flow down to the mill 3 miles distant, which would in turn allow the mill wheel to turn, which would then solve the problem. Well, the hole they dug was in quicksand, and the whole earth gave way. It caused a massive flood from here to Newport [about 15 miles north]. How could that show be offensive? Just politics, I guess."

Sunday afternoons are primo for B&P Theater. Two hours earlier, a volunteer had directed me to one of the overflow parking lots about a quarter mile from the museum. (Usually, I was told, there was more than enough room to park down on the Circus Field.) At a tour of the museum with thirty other guests, conducted by staff member Rose Friedman, I learn that the huge, 140-year-old hay barn housing the museum has undergone extensive reconstruction over the past year to neutralize its sinking slowly into the ground, and that the state has pitched in to help save this excellent example of agricultural architecture. On two levels of the barn are housed the thousands of papier-mâché and cardboard puppets—carved, painted, and molded—that have been used over the years, and that are resurrected as needed for present-day productions. Rose describes their context, as well as their functions.

Later Linda goes over the day's schedule. "After the circus we have a pageant. And after that we're doing an old street show called *Hallelujah*. And then after that a friend of ours from the Awareness Theater Company in Burlington is doing two presentations over there," she says, pointing to a building on the other side of the street. "Sundays are pretty full."

Bread and Puppet circuses incorporate political satire, dancing, music, parades, and sideshows that isolate one of the several themes for that particular circus, but also include material independent of any particular project's theme.

In addition to the Glover summer schedule, B&P maintains rigorous fall, winter, and spring tours dominated by visits to college campuses, churches, elementary schools, museums, galleries, theaters and town halls, centering on one region each season. Their most recent fall schedule included colleges, high schools, and communities in North Carolina, Georgia, and Virginia, winding up in New York City during late November and December for Divine Reality Circus and Pageant performances over the holidays. The international schedule for any given year could be as diverse as, say, Haiti, Italy, and Canada.

Directions: The theater is south of Glover Village about 1 mile on Route 122, at 753 Heights Road. During July and August, the troupe performs on the Glover grounds Friday evenings and Sunday afternoons. There usually is a mid- to late-June celebration of the museum opening, and afternoon performances in October, the annual political leaf peeping. Performances are free, but donations are welcome. The museum is open June through October, 10:00 a.m. to 5:00 p.m. daily. No admission required, but donations are encouraged. Call (802) 525-1271 for details or visit www. breadandpuppet.org

YOUTUBE VIDEO:
"Vermont's BREAD & PUPPET THEATER - WildTravelsTV.com" (6:22)
(Elka Schumann interview and tour of the barn) 🍁

MUSEUM OF EVERYDAY LIFE

Glover

Gabriel Levine

Museum of Everyday Life curators encourage visitors to not just observe but also participate in collecting objects and contributing personal stories about them.

If you can't read the subtitle in the museum exterior photo, let me help. It goes, "embarking on our mission of glorious obscurity." This is a joyous statement of fact and perhaps also a progress report, unless founder and curator Clare Dolan wants obscurity to be a destination—rather than an early stage in the lengthy duration of the Museum of Everyday Life. We're betting on the latter.

Clare started with a simple but pure vision: What if there was a museum dedicated to exploring, analyzing and celebrating everyday life objects, rather than the exotic, the endangered, the extinct or the obsolete? What if there were not only no "do not touch" signs, but guests instead were encouraged to be co-creators of the museum—not just observing but participating in the collection of objects and contributing their personal stories.

Full appreciation of MOEL's exhibits requires a slower, and much more thorough and detailed observation—tracing often surprising and fascinating origins, uses, and perspectives. The first four Clare chose to carry this burden were the match, the safety pin, the pencil and the tooth brush.

"I knew right away the object I'd choose first was the match," says Clare. "It seemed so perfect: tiny, powerful, and symbolic. I love its action; that it holds in itself this burst of light and heat. It's both an exciting and dangerous object in its association with fire, warmth, revolution and other forms of transformation—of food, for example.

"The safety pin to me embodied the power and aura exactly the opposite of the match. "Healing Engine of Emergency" was the title of the safety pin exhibit—taken from that beautiful Christopher Morley essay, and which I posted as part of the exhibit. I am completely captivated by their simple, elegant shapes and their gorgeous utility.

"These two "ordinary" objects, as well as the pencil and the toothbrush, have gone through a number of "improvements" (for the match, the lighter; for the safety pin, Velcro; etc.), but the mechanical, low-tech, original item remains ubiquitous. Somehow these articles are so elemental they won't go away. We can't do without them!"

The Museum's Exhibits and Collections is but one of three MOEL components. The Philosophy Department keeps things humming on a conceptual level, producing all necessary theoretical tracts, curatorial methodologies, and encyclopedism. More information as it becomes available. The Museum's Performance Company creates puppet shows and performances to further examine everyday life through the "lives" of objects. As a longtime performer with the Bread & Puppet Theater, Clare brings professional experience at an international level to this activity.

In the winter Clare conducts workshops in nearby public schools. The first of these was an Albany Community School program where over a six-week period, kids from grades 1-6 created their own miniature museums after school.

Now keep in mind in addition to all this, Clare is an intensive care nurse at a St. Johnsbury hospital. Not only that—when, between the match and the safety pin exhibits her house next to MOEL burned to the ground, a cast of supportive friends helped her rebuild it.

Now there's a plucky curator. Continued good luck, Clare!

From the South - Take U.S. I-91 North to Vermont exit 24 and turn North onto VT Rt 122. Follow 122 through the small villages of Wheelock and Sheffield, and continue, past the Bread and Puppet Theater, until Rt 122 terminates at VT RT16. Turn Left (South) onto Rt 16 and drive aprx. 5 miles until you see a small pond on your right. The Museum is the first structure immediately following the pond.

From the North - Take U.S. I-91 South to Vermont exit 25 and turn South onto VT Rt 16. Drive through the small village of Glover, past Red Sky Trading and Currier's Market, and continue about 5.5 miles until you see a small pond on your right. The Museum is the first structure immediately following the pond, at 3482 Dry Pond Rd., Glover, VT 05839YouTube Video:

YOUTUBE VIDEO:
"Answers to Four Questions" (6:10)
(The Museum curator in performance) ♣

PARKER PIE, FINAL DESTINATION ON AN IDEAL SUNDAY

I have the perfect Sunday planned, whether you're coming north on I-91 or working your way south from the Canadian border. Not any Sunday, though. Ideally, this will be a fine June, July, August, or September Sunday. So far so good? Let's say you happen to be in or near St. Johnsbury within this month-frame, are having breakfast there or nearby, and have an open mind about the rest of the day, as well. Ready? 1): The Fairbanks Museum and Planetarium (p. 196) opens at nine, so you can spend a couple of hours there; 2): Maybe take in a smoothie or snack there before the half-hour trip north to 3): Glover's Museum of Everyday Things (see directions above). MOEL will demand at least an hour of your time—maybe more. Just be sure to leave in time for 4): The 3 p.m. performance at the Bread and Puppet Theater (directions just above those of MOEL. It will be worth It in spades. Then It's time for 5): a scrumptious meal at the Parker Pie Co. just eight minutes away, as follows: Head northwest on VT-122 N toward Old Heights Rd for .7 mi.; turn right onto VT-16 N 1.4 mi.; left onto Bean Hill Rd. for 2.5 mi.; then continue onto County Rd. for .2 mi, and PPC will be on your left. For the record, I know no one there and am not steering you there for any reason other than to tell you just know how tasty and memorable the food, service, and atmosphere were the one time we tried It. After checking out the poignant home page at parkerpie.com, move on to a complete description of their famous pizzas and other specialties. additional questions? Call 802.525.3366.

BRUTAL RAID ON AN ABENAKI VILLAGE

Granby

On a mountaintop just beyond a log house a mile north of Granby, a 10-foot-by-12-foot split-rail-fenced cemetery holds two graves, each graced with a small American flag. Nearby, a granite bench awaits the rare visitor who comes to pay homage.

No way would I have found this place without the help of Joe Benning, a Lyndonville attorney with an interest in colonial history, who has kindly taken the afternoon off to show me the grave sites and give me a tour of the area. "This is the final resting place of two of the famed Rogers' Rangers," says Joe. A plaque inside the split rail fence verifies this.

Major Robert Rogers was a New Hampshire farmer recruited in 1755 by the British for service in the French and Indian War. This was back in the days when New York occupied some of the territory that is now Vermont, and New Hampshire claimed it as well. In 1759, Rogers was ordered by British general Jeffrey Amherst to leave Crown Point, New York, and attack the Abenaki village of Odanak, on the Saint Francis River in Canada. This was a revenge attack, in retaliation for the Abenaki's longtime alliance with the French, and for a recent raid on a retreating British unit.

The Abenaki at Odanak (also called Saint Francis) had been celebrating an excellent hunting and gathering harvest that fall, dancing and feasting well into the night. The main body of Rogers's unit—about 150 men—waited 3 miles from the village while two scouts kept watch. About a half hour before dawn, after the entire village had retired, Rogers and his men attacked. Three hours later, up to 200 men, women, and children were dead, and smoking ruins were all that remained of nearly all the sixty or more frame houses and a Jesuit mission church. Only about one hundred Abenaki are thought to have survived.

About a week after their retreat from Odanak, the Rangers broke into small groups somewhere near Lake Memphremagog on the U.S.-Canadian border. Their destination was Fort Number 4, at Charlestown, New Hampshire, on the Connecticut River. At least three groups of Rangers came down through what is now the Northeast Kingdom. Many of them had little room for food in their packs, having looted the church in Odanak of silver-plated copper chandeliers, "massive" golden candlesticks, and a solid silver statuette of Our Lady of Chartres inlaid with a ruby "as big as an eyeball." Other sources also mention bags of silver and gold coins.

But here's where the stories get confusing. Most agree that as hunger took its toll, the men gradually discarded their plunder, most marking their hiding places for retrieval later. The two soldiers who got as far as Granby, however, just 20 miles from the Connecticut River, are said to have been killed either by wolves who disputed their ownership of a killed moose, or by Abenaki who trailed and finally caught up with them.

"In either case," says Joe Benning, "I don't know how you could prove it at this late date without exhuming the remains."

Directions: To reach the grave sites, take I-91 exit 23; then travel on U.S. Route 5 through Lyndonville approximately 2 miles to Route 114. Then go another 3 miles to a fork at which Route 114 bears left, and Victory Road (not marked) goes right. Take the right. Go another 3 miles to Granby, and take the first left, Porrell Road. At the top of the mountain, just past a log house, are the fenced grave sites on the left ❧

KINGDOM COUNTY PRODUCTIONS—HELLO TO VOLLYWOOD!

Peacham

Vermont's Northeast Kingdom is the film capital of northern New England. In addition to feature films and documentaries, it offers an additional bonus, or perhaps legacy. Whatever you call it, Bess O'Brien and Jay Craven have found a way to seed, nurture, and harvest a continual crop of formative stage and screen pros, behind and in front of both camera and proscenium. True, this is not the principal mission at Kingdom County Productions, but it is an organic outgrowth.

Bess gives me an example one fall afternoon as we sit on a side porch of the couple's Peacham home, overlooking a wide swath of the Connecticut River valley. (Jay was in Africa and Asia at the time, part of a cultural exchange on behalf of the State Department and the National Endowment of the Arts, talking to independent filmmakers about *Disappearance,* a recent film,)

Bess O'Brien and Jay Craven examine a film script—a good one, from their expressions—at their home in Peacham.

"About fifteen years ago, Blue Cross/Blue Shield of Vermont asked me to create a project based on the lives of Vermont teenagers—the hook being the health of kids in the state," says Bess, working on a late lunch of cheese and crackers. "I came up with the idea of an original musical, along the lines of *Fame*. We spent about eight months all over Vermont, using workshops to learn about the lives of kids from all walks of life. Then we put together a script based on the kids we had met."

Bess and co-producer/co-writer Abby Paige then brought in a number of talented teenagers to write the original music. The finished piece, a theater production called *Voices*, toured in thirteen towns all over Vermont. It was a big sensation, to the extent that Bess turned it into a screenplay and an independent film under the Kingdom County Productions (KCP) banner. A more extended tour of the film—to fifty towns in Vermont—was followed by submissions to international film festivals and a tour of New England.

"I edited that film with an editor I worked with on one of my documentaries. She was a student of Jay's who also taught at Marlboro College. She graduated years ago and has worked her way up. Her name is Carrie Sterr, and she's terrific. Through the years We end up hiring a lot of Jay's students who graduate from Marlboro.

"For *Voices* that summer we used a lot of interns—film students from Marlboro, Burlington College, Keene State—so they got a chance to work with mentors, not getting paid, but learning a lot. So it's a great thing for their résumés and they get a lot of experience." To bring it full circle, Carrie served as film-editing mentor to the students interested in her chosen field.

The other option KCP has for young people interested in a film career is its Fledgling Films arm, organized in 1997 to give young people hands-on experience in media arts production. One Fledgling student directed an off-Broadway play last summer and spent the fall semester shooting two films. Another graduate of the Fledgling Summer Institute started his own youth film festival.

Despite minuscule budgets compared to those at Hollywood-studio level—that happens to be what KCP can afford, after all—the studio attracts such top-dollar talent as Rip Torn, Martin Sheen, Michael J. Fox, Geneviève Bujold, and Kris Kristofferson.

"Michael J. Fox was terrific," says Bess. "He was living in Vermont at the time, and it was one of those things—we knew the guy who was working on his house. He told Michael there were filmmakers in the Northeast Kingdom who wanted to meet him." Fox watched *High Water,* was impressed, met Jay and Bess, and agreed to be in *Where the Rivers Flow North,* which also starred Rip Torn and Tantoo Cardinal.

"Because he was shooting another movie in Canada at the time, it was difficult trying to get through to his manager. For managers and agents it's all about the money, and protecting their clients from all the people who want them to do every project in the world. But you never know. With Kris we *did* go through his agent, and it worked out. Kris called here one day out of the blue and read the script [for *Disappearances*] and loved it. He said, 'I'm committed to this project for however long it takes.' It took five years from that phone call to get the money together. But he hung in there."

So why do stars of this caliber work with KCP for so little money, comparatively?

"I think they do it because a lot of the roles they are asked to do give them a lot of money but aren't challenging to them. I think Kris, for example, although he does a lot of commercial work, saw this as a terrific role to play as an older man. In an independent film you can take more risks, and it's not all about the money. Plus Jay's a fine director and the scripts are really strong.

"Ours are rural films with minimal national distribution power. They're like vaudeville. We make them and then we tour them from town to town. Not that it will make anyone a lot of money, but that it's a good thing to do, enriches the region, and disseminates a film to its own culture in a way that reflects Vermont and otherwise would not be out there."

Bess also produced *Coming Home,* a documentary focused on five people returning to their Vermont communities from prison. The film focuses on the Innovative Circle of Support and Accountability, which helps reintegrate former prisoners back into the community. The film premiered in the fall of 2018 and subsequently toured Vermont.

"Bess O'Brien and Kingdom County Productions' work Is exemplary in the state of Vermont," said Senator Bernie Sanders, "and has raised issues that are critical to children and families."

For a detailed look at the history of Kingdom County Productions, its critically acclaimed films, and its current and upcoming activities, see www.kingdomcounty.com.

YOUTUBE VIDEOS:
"Kingdom County Productions"
(More than a dozen to choose from) ✤

VERMONT EDUCATOR, LEGISLATOR, AND HISTORIAN WITHOUT PEER

Saint Johnsbury

Nine months after this photo was taken, Graham Newell died at 92. Colleagues admired his "bear-trap mind." Graham lauded his students' triumphs and sublimated his own.

"No, not there. To the right. Down one shelf. Yes. There it is."

I'm in Graham Newell's St. Johnsbury study on a sunny Sunday September afternoon. He is sharing a little historical gossip and directing me to Calvin Coolidge's autobiography from his armchair across the room. Graham, 92, uses a walker to get around but still teaches intermediate Latin in his home three times weekly to a dozen St. Johnsbury Academy students.

Coolidge was rejected at Amherst, Graham tells me, because the academic standards at his school, Black River Academy, were too low. But Amherst's administrators agreed that if Coolidge came to St. Johnsbury Academy and made decent grades for a year, they would admit him.

Graham asks me to read the Coolidge account: "After a few weeks in the winter at my old school, I went to St. Johnsbury Academy for the spring term. Its principal was Dr. Putney . . . a very exact scholar and an excellent disciplinarian. He readily gave me a certificate entitling me to enter Amherst without further examination, which he would never have done if he had not been convinced I was a proficient student."

"Oh, that's Coolidge for you," says Graham, chortling.

Back to the printed account: "[Dr. Putney's] endorsement of [my work] . . . showed that Black River Academy was not without some merit."

"When he wrote this thirty years later, though," says Graham with obvious glee, "Black River Academy was flourishing. So you can see he doesn't tell you the whole story—that Black River Academy couldn't get him into Amherst!"

Graham Newell is seventh-generation Saint Johnsbury, and the town's honorary ambassador. "People send people who move here to me when they want to quickly know the history of our town." He shows me the genealogical cheat sheet he has prepared for such occurrences. "You've got to memorize the names of the three Fairbanks brothers at the top there: Thaddeus, inventor of the scale; Erastus, governor twice of Vermont; and their brother, Joseph, who died young but had one son who built the house next to me, and who wrote a history of the town of Saint Johnsbury."

Graham started teaching English, Latin, and then history at Saint Johnsbury Academy after graduating from the University of Chicago in 1938. (He later returned for his master's degree in Latin and completed course work for his Ph.D.) In 1953 Newell ran successfully for the Vermont legislature and served in both the house and senate for twenty-six years—twenty of them as chairman of the senate education committee—while maintaining his position as head of the history department at Lyndon State College. Because the legislature didn't meet on Mondays, Graham conducted classes on campus those days. On Wednesdays and Fridays he climbed up to the "crow's nest" of the Capitol Dome in Montpelier and communicated with his history students through a long-distance telephone hookup called a telelecture. An assistant at Lyndon State transmitted student questions back to Graham. As a legislator Graham is proudest of two bills he wrote and prodded to passage in the late 1950s. The Fair Dismissal for Teachers bill guarantees that no teacher can be fired without a hearing. His Special Education bill was the first legislation nationwide to establish a public school curriculum, grades K–12, for students with special needs. Graham voted as an "Aiken Republican," the liberal wing of the party, but today considers himself an Independent.

In 1962 Graham recalls being summoned from the Senate floor for a call from the White House. "President Kennedy's right-hand man told me the President had just appointed me a member of the Advisory Commission on Intergovernmental Relations. The Commission consisted—as it does today—of two members of every body of government at national, state, county, and municipal levels–about 24 members in all. Graham, one of two state legislators selected nationwide, met with his colleagues once a month in Washington. "Senator Sam Ervin [later Chairman of the Watergate Commission] was chairman of the entire commission, and I got to know him very well. In October 1963 we were told that JFK had invited us to meet with him at the White House for our December 1 meeting. One month later he was dead. That was the most tragic of my few brushes with what I call fame.

"At the moment," says Graham, "I'm disposing of a lot of my books and historical documents. I have hundreds, going back to the eighteenth century. I thought of giving them to the University of Vermont. I received an honorary doctorate there a couple of years ago. The Vermont Historical Society was a possibility, as well. I was president there from 1964 to 1969. But I've decided that everything will go across the street to the Newell Collection, in the academy's archive room."

Only fitting, it seems, that one of the rare *living* icons to have a building named for him—Newell Hall, in this case—would trust his most prized possessions to an institution that in turn values him so highly.

Directions: Take exit 20 on I-91. At the end of the exit ramp, turn right, and take the next left up the hill. When the road levels out, you will be on Main Street and at the Saint Johnsbury Academy campus. For more information visit www.stjohnsburyacademy.org. ✤

13,555 BEETLES AND BUTTERFLIES DIED FOR THIS ARTISTIC EXPERIMENT

Saint Johnsbury

public domain

"Completed in 1897," reads the plaque, "and honoring the Articles
of Confederation and perpetual union created in 1777." Yes, those
13,555 coleoptera and lepidoptera gladly gave it up for their
country, and we thank them for it.

Given the title of this book, you shouldn't be surprised that in a few rare instances we've taken what one might call the low road. Clearly, a certain number of curiosities have driven us there. Let's face it—that's just the nature of the "Who Knew" business. I say this to assure you that the Fairbanks Museum "bug art" exhibit described a few paragraphs from here is far from representative of the high standards maintained elsewhere in the building.

We begin by reintroducing Erastus Fairbanks from the previous entry, whose son Franklin founded the Fairbanks Museum. Franklin Fairbanks, who became president of the scale company started by his uncle Thaddeus, wanted to give something back to the community. What better gift than a three-level museum that he could seed with exhibits from his own vast personal collection, which he called his "cabinet of curiosities." Our kind of guy! It became a reality in 1889. Following is a brief tour.

Lower Floor. The Fairbanks Museum and Planetarium (its full name) has maintained a weather observation site in its basement ever since 1894, largely because Franklin Fairbanks kept meticulous weather records in his Saint Johnsbury home. It seemed natural for him to make the weather bureau—and ultimately the planetarium—a permanent part of the museum.

Meteorologists Mark Breen and Steve Maleski have broadcast eight or more daily weather forecasts over Vermont Public Radio since 1981. Rookie Lawrence Hayes joined them in 2008. Their comprehensive analyses go far beyond customary "cloudy today, sunny tomorrow" 30-second TV reports. "Our focus is basically the North American continent and surrounding areas," says Breen, "because it directly impacts [Vermont] weather. A storm track out in the Pacific during the typhoon season, for example, has an effect on storms that eventually reach Alaska, which in turn affects the weather pattern across North America. Covering that broad an area encompasses most of the factors that affect us five or six days from now, which we discuss in a general sense. Then we look in more detail at regions closer to us, to talk about the impact over the next forty-eight hours."

As you might also guess, there is a tribute to the Fairbanks platform scale that made all of this possible. It's on display just a few feet down from the Snowflake Bentley exhibit (you'll read about him a few paragraphs down), courtesy of the museum's founder's uncle Thaddeus, who not only invented it but distributed it worldwide, to China, Russia, Cuba, India, and much of Europe. By 1897 the company held 113 patents for inventions and improvements in weighing accuracy.

Main Floor. The ground floor is dominated by 75,000 mounted birds, reptiles, mammals, and fish. Franklin was also an amateur naturalist, and some of the birds he shot became part of the extensive "Birds and Animals of the World" display. Taxidermist William

Balch did the stuffing and mounting, as well as some of the shooting. Two pair of now-extinct passenger pigeons are included, as well as a collection of 131 species of hummingbirds, thought to be the largest such collection in North America.

Upper Level. Now. Ah yes, the bug art. The perpetrator of these works is John Hampson, who at one time worked as a mechanical engineer for Thomas Edison in New Jersey and in his spare time arranged dead insects into shapes depicting historical events. The one that took 13,555 butterflies and beetles (and several years) to complete was a representation of Old Glory honoring the Articles of Confederation. Others include *Abraham Lincoln's Proclamation of Freedom, General Pershing on His Horse,* and *Washington Bidding His Generals Goodbye.* When Hampson died, his daughter trolled a number of museums pleading for bug-art perpetuity, with the Fairbanks finally agreeing to display the nine works. The upper level (balcony) also leads to the planetarium.

Directions: Take I-91 exit 20 (U.S. Route 5/Railroad Street) and go north to Main Street. Go left up the hill 2 blocks beyond the stop sign. The museum is on the right, at 1302 Main. Museum hours and planetarium showings vary by season. For more information call (802) 748-2372, or better yet, visit the museum's website at www.fairbanks.museum.org, where a virtual tour is even available, though the real thing is much better.

YOUTUBE VIDEO:
"Fairbanks Museum Opens New Digital Planetarium" (2:11) 2012 Vermont Public Radio video, hosted by meteorologist Mark Breen) ♣

FARMER PHOTOGRAPHS WORLD'S FIRST SNOWFLAKE

"Somebody had to photograph the first snowflake," reads the exhibit plaque at Saint Johnsbury's Fairbanks Museum. We heartily concur. Wilson "Snowflake" Bentley was a Vermont treasure, as unique as the snow crystals he captured as microphotographs.

A self-educated farmer from Jericho, he invented the process of microphotography using a microscope and camera. He went on to capture over 5,000 images of snow crystals from 1885 until his death in 1931. In addition, he studied formations of frost, dew, and raindrops in great detail. He also conducted some of the first research in cloud physics.

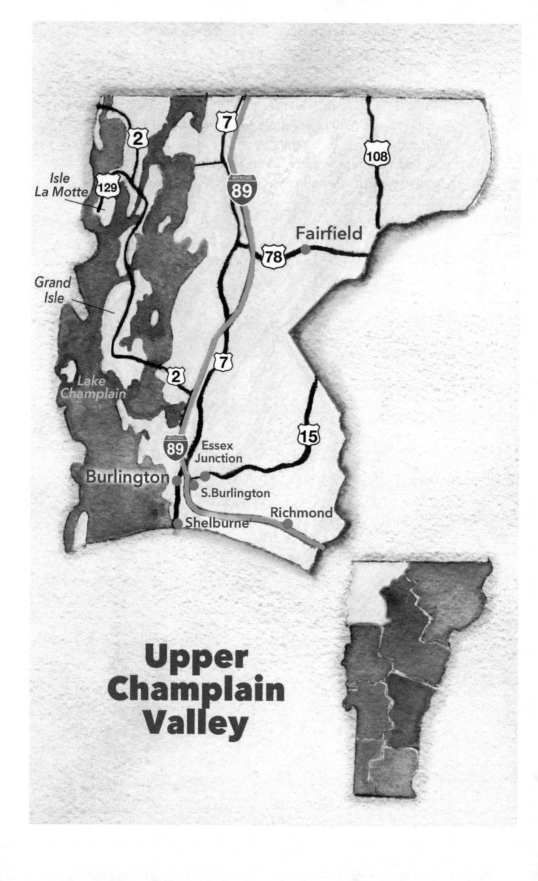

Upper
Champlain
Valley

9

UPPER CHAMPLAIN VALLEY

Only about 110 miles long and 12 miles wide, most folks wouldn't think to call Lake Champlain an actual "Great Lake." Yet for one week it came close to achieving such national renown. The intent was simply to make Vermont schools eligible to receive "Sea Grant funding" by adding Lake Champlain to the list of Great Lakes already being funded. Instead, some Midwesterners were outraged. A New York Times *story claimed that Vermont Senator Patrick Leahy had slipped seven additional words into the bill: "The term Great Lakes includes Lake Champlain." We got us a brouhaha! But it all turned out well, as you'll see.*

Senator Leahy also had a hand in establishing ECHO Lake Aquarium and Science Center—Vermont's best location to study "Ecology, Culture, History, and Opportunity." But it was Country Home *magazine that named Burlington tops among all U.S. cities for "Best Green Places," followed by an unfortunate caveat.*

YOUTUBE VIDEO:
"Top 14 Tourist Attractions In Burlington - Travel Vermont" (2:10)
(Excellent preview covering most of the Upper Champlain Valley)

ECHO ... ECHO ... ECHO ... LAKE AQUARIUM AND SCIENCE CENTER

Burlington

Look at that cute little guy saying "come on in!" One passerby was heard to say as she looked at the window painting: "I think the drawing is fabulous. It just looks airy and inviting."

Just before you set foot in ECHO, a fine mist sprayed between slabs of lake slate bathes the air on both sides of the two-story glass entrance. I saw dancing rainbows, but that can't always happen, can it? Even if not, it sure is a good mood-setter.

This estimable establishment is called "ECHO Leahy Center for Lake Champlain." ECHO stands for ecology, culture, history, and opportunity—a mouthful that is also quite accurate. It is named in honor of Vermont's U.S. senator Patrick Leahy and his wife, Marcelle. Senator Leahy raised $7.5 million—more than half the building's total cost—from three federal agencies to build the waterfront center.

These cute little guys are part of a program ECHO Is running with the VT Fish & Wildlife Dept. to give spiny softshell turtles a head start on life in Lake Champlain.

ECHO uses the term "One Drop" to share its mission with visitors and the community. The organization believes everyone is capable of one drop—metaphorically, one good deed—to help create a lasting ripple effect. ECHO knows one drop is all It takes to change an action, change a mind, and change the world. Its "One Drop" motto shows that anyone can make a difference,

"All of the content and all of exhibits work together," says Julie Silverman, former director of New (as in innovative, visionary ideas). "In 1995 we took over an old naval reserve building that was on this site. We stayed there for six years until plans for the new building were in place. Two years later, in 2003, we moved in.

"Anything we could salvage from the old building, we did. The boards we're standing on are Douglas fir timbers from the old building, replaned, remilled, and put in as decking." This example of reclamation is but one of dozens of ecological decisions that led to ECHO being the first Vermont building certified by the U.S.

Green Building Council the year it opened. Other criteria for this rating include energy use and renewal, environmental impact, and waste management and recycling.

ECHO's most recent addition brings a unique 3-D movie experience to Vermont. The Northfield Savings Bank Theater, a National Geographic Experience, is the only theater of its kind in the state. It brings to ECHO guests all year-round the incredible National Geographic films that many of them know and love.

Julie sums up the philosophy behind the many attractions at ECHO, including the more than seventy species of live fish, amphibians, and reptiles. "We are very much place based," she says. "Most of the content and exhibits are about the Lake Champlain basin. We give people an opportunity to see species they would never see otherwise—the sturgeon, for example, because that type of historic animal has been around as long as the dinosaurs."

According to Julie, that information usually elicits one of two follow-up questions, particularly from school groups: "*That* lives in Lake Champlain?" or "*That* fish is as old as a dinosaur?"

"Yes," of course, is the answer to the first question. As to the second, guides proclaim, usually on a daily basis, "No, we're not talking about *that particular sturgeon*. We're saying the sturgeon species has been around as long as the dinosaurs!"

The sturgeon and other major fish exhibits are downstairs in the under-the-lake exhibit. Frogs, turtles, newts, and other aboveground creatures live upstairs.

ECHO's Action Lab, which opened in 2013, brings to visitors new ways to see the environment. This hands-on wing is geared toward older learners and those interested in citizen science and looking to make a difference. The augmented reality sandbox, demonstrating how watersheds develop, is a guest favorite. There are time-lapse videos to show lake conditions, and a virtual boat tour around the basin.

Finally, remember Champ the Lake Champlain monster, from Chapter 1? The folks at ECHO are here to tell you they have photographic proof that he—and or she—actually inhabit(s) the lake. The photo, taken by Vermonter Sandra Mansi, is not always displayed though, so if you're interested and don't see it, ask a staff member to amplify. (Speculation aside: Seems to me unless our elusive varmint has a life span of at least 150 years, we should be talking about a Mom *and* Pop Champ. Just sayin'.)

Allow plenty of time to explore and enjoy ECHO. Trying to cover in a single day the wealth of information and surprises available is overly ambitious. Try planning your trip in advance by reviewing the website.

Directions: Enter Burlington on U.S. Route 2, which becomes Main Street. Turn north onto Battery Street. Drive 1 block and take a left at the light onto College Street. ECHO is located at the bottom of College Street on the waterfront. Hours vary by season and special exhibits change frequently, so check ahead. For more information, visit www.echovermont.org or call (802) 864-1848.

YOUTUBE VIDEOS:
"ECHO Lake Aquarium and Science Center" (3:35)
(Comprehensive Narrated Tour)

"Big Fish Feeding at Echo Lake Aquarium and Science Center" (5:29)
(To be clear, that's not only fish-feeding and feeding fish, but also feeding fish to fish)

"Spirit of Ethan Allen Via Aerial" (1:40)
(A drone's-eye view of the Burlington waterfront) ✤

LAKE CHAMPLAIN—HONORARY GREAT LAKE FOR A WEEK

Burlington

On March 5, 1998, President Bill Clinton signed Senate Bill 927, written primarily to reauthorize the Sea Grant Program, which deals with the study of environmental issues concerning states that border the Great Lakes and states with coastlines. This legislation incidentally recognized Lake Champlain as the nation's sixth Great Lake, along with Lakes Superior, Ontario, Michigan, Erie, and Huron,

These Lake Champlain swimmers don't care about being in a Great Lake. They just know it's a great lake.

for purposes of projects and funding. One week later, the Great Lakes Commission (a binational U.S. and state agency dedicated to promoting a healthy environment for the Great Lakes–Saint Lawrence region) decreed that Lake Champlain was no longer a Great Lake. What happened?

During that week—and for months thereafter—the contention was that Senator Patrick Leahy was trying to pull a fast one. The American Geological Institute referred to an amendment by Senator Leahy "to include Lake Champlain as one of the Great Lakes . . . in order for schools in Vermont to receive Sea Grant funding." A *New York Times* story claimed that Senator Leahy slipped seven words into the bill: "'The term Great Lakes includes Lake Champlain'—and thus unleashed a storm of protest in the Middle West."

Ohio senator John Glenn adapted a quote from an earlier Lloyd Bentsen–Dan Quayle vice presidential debate: "I know the Great Lakes. I've traveled to the Great Lakes. And Lake Champlain is not one of the Great Lakes."

The only accurate part of these accusations was that the senator did indeed want the University of Vermont to be able to compete for National Sea Grant College status. "The arguments for [Lake Champlain] being very similar [to the Great Lakes] in almost all regards except total area is pretty strong," said Dr. Larry Forcier, director of the Lake Champlain Sea Grant program at the University of Vermont.

But even so, Senator Leahy never requested that Lake Champlain be added as the sixth Great Lake, only that it be eligible for Sea Grant money. Bob Paquin, a Vermont aide to Senator Leahy, recalls it this way: "The words Senator Leahy added to the bill after the words 'shall include the Great Lakes' were '[comma] and Lake Champlain.' But agencies affected by the legislation are customarily invited to comment on bill language, and in this case it was the National Oceanic and Atmospheric Administration. NOAA officials asked that Senator Leahy's wording be changed to include Lake Champlain in the definition of the Great Lakes watershed."

Paquin agrees with Larry Forcier regarding Lake Champlain's qualifications for receiving Sea Grant funding. "Among scientists there's no debate on the hydrology," he said. "We are part of the Great Lakes–Saint Lawrence system. So including the canal system—Champlain, Hudson River, and Erie—in terms of invasive species, for example, whatever they get, we get."

So the Leahy team went along with that language because it accomplished its goal. But then a Midwest news organization picked up an article in the *Burlington, Vermont, Free Press* about the Sea Grant funding provision and the reworked NOAA language, and in one day it was all over the country that Lake Champlain had been declared a Great Lake. Reporters searched their Rolodexes (absent Bing or Google as yet) to find geologists for interviews about the controversy.

Midwestern lawmakers, when asked back home whether they had been asleep at the switch, reacted with indignation. With a bit of egg on its face, the Michigan-based Great Lakes Commission on March 11 opposed the designation of Lake Champlain as a "Great Lake." Within days the Senate unanimously passed Leahy's compromise, adding Lake Champlain to Sea Grant eligibility status, and listing it as "among the Great Lakes natural resources."

The Sea Grant people were delighted with the publicity. Senator Leahy and his staff accomplished their mission. And the State University of New York at Plattsburgh was a benefactor as well, happy to join the Sea Grant team by virtue of its location on the west side of Lake Champlain.

"The Senator found the whole sequence amusing," said Bob Paquin. "We like to say that Lake Champlain is still 'great' to us—and after all, if you take 1776 into account, it is this country's *first* great lake." In any case, scientists on both sides of the lake will now be able to conduct research to help solve its problems, eradicating the zebra mussel and other invasive species, for example, which affect the five other Great Lakes, as well. ◆

CULTURAL MAGNET FOR A COMMUNITY

Burlington

Back in 1930 John J. Flynn built the Flynn Theatre strictly for vaude-ville. With its huge proscenium arch—largest in the state—future backstage expansion definitely was an option. In the interim the Golden Age of Hollywood came calling, which meant adapting that proscenium to accommodate a fixed screen for the first of the talkies. For a brief time thereafter, a movable screen accommodated both film and performance art. Then the Flynn made its complete break. Despite a relatively low population base, new ownership counted on growing community interest to support its total commitment to live theater, music, and dance. After a complete renovation in 1981, the Flynn Center for the Performing Arts was born. Its inaugural concert in an all-live-all-the-time format included the Vermont Symphony Orchestra and a number of area artists.

Since that time several additional renovations have made the Flynn the region's leading performance center, now run by local community leaders as a nonprofit organization. It is recognized internationally (Canada is only an hour away) for its artistic activities, its superb technical capacity, and its world-class presentations. In any given month the main stage hosts road companies from Japan to Nebraska, and performances are often sold out well before opening night.

We didn't promise the book would be commercial-free—call this an unintended consequence.

Throughout its frequent makeovers the physical plant's art deco integrity has been scrupulously preserved. On a tour of the house, facilities director Jack Galt points out the meticulous application of a thin line of gold paint to the wrought iron railings. It enhances a three-dimensional effect that visitors will appreciate, if only subconsciously.

What separates the Flynn from most other commercial live-performance theaters, though, is the extent of its community outreach, which takes several forms. There are performing arts classes, for example, embracing an array of acting, dance, and music classes for one-year-olds, ninety-year-olds, and all in between. There's voice for teens and adults, ballet, directing for the stage, jazz combo, stand-up comedy, hip-hop, rhythm tap, junior creative dance, and a dozen more. Also scheduled are one-time evening and weekend workshops and programs to help educators improve their creative arts teaching skills.

In 1997 the Flynn was part of a gala community fund-raising bash, in concert with the legendary Vermont rock band Phish and entrepreneurs Ben Cohen and Jerry Greenfield—better known as the founders of Ben & Jerry's ice cream. B&J had created a flavor called Phish Food in honor of the band (later spun off as the popular chocolate-covered ice cream bar Phish Sticks). To simultaneously kick off the release of this ice cream flavor and to validate the environmental awareness of both B&J and the band, 100 percent of the royalties from the license of Phish Food were funneled into Waterwheel, the band's nonprofit organization. Through Waterwheel, all such funds are used to clean up the Lake Champlain watershed from industrial, urban, and agricultural runoff. The concert was a sellout.

Directions: Coming in on U.S. Route 2, which turns into Main Street, the Flynn Center is at 153 Main, just west of the Burlington City Hall. For more information about the center or for tickets, visit www.flynncenter.org, or call (802) 86-FLYNN.

YOUTUBE VIDEO:
"Flynn Center for the Performing Arts: PTV Award Winner" (2:21) (Detailed look at 2014 complete renovation)

BEST OF THE "BEST GREEN PLACES"

According to *Country Home* magazine in Its first "Best Green Places" survey rating U.S. cities on the basis of air and watershed quality, mass-transit use, power use, and number of organic farmers and farmers' markets, Burlington, Vermont was rated number one out of the 379 U.S. metropolitan areas listed.

Burlington rated high marks for:

- A compost that collects food scraps from restaurants and supermarkets and sells them to farmers and gardeners

- Its sixteen farmers' markets, five organic producers, and three co-ops.

- The 12.3 percent of Its commuters who carpool, the 5.6 percent of Its workforce who walk to work, and the 4.6 percent who work at home.

Top rankings of adjacent states among the 379 listed:

Ithaca, NY	2
Springfield, MA	4
Portland, ME	34
Rockingham and Stratford Counties, NH	187

Unfortunately, because *Country Home* ceased publication in 2009 (the following year), no-one knows how many consecutive times Burlington might have continued to receive this prestigious honor. (Best guess after polling VT Who Knew Survey Committee: Ten.)

A 25,000-MILE, IN-STATE STROLL

Essex Junction

The 251 Club Wayfarer is a newsletter for Vermonters intent on visiting all 251 of the state's towns and cities. *Wayfarer* editor Bill Rockford gave me a paragraph in one edition to ask members about their unusual experiences. One response stood out by far.

Dr. Edward Keenan had never set out to log all 251 Vermont communities. Only after he received a gift membership did he and his wife begin attending meetings. Following are a few of Dr. Keenan's recollections:

"Many of my early long walks had to do with the American Lung Association's annual 100-mile Bike Treks. I would start about 2 a.m., many miles before the first cyclists passed me. My longest one-day walk was 89 miles, completed in 23 hours, 20 minutes. My longest multi-day walk started at the Massachusetts border and ended at the Canadian border four days later.

"I took seats out of my van to convert it to a mobile home. By careful planning I mapped out circle routes to begin and end where the van was parked. On a 78-mile walk from Bradford to Burlington to benefit the Fanny Allen Hospital, one of the nuns walked with me from the airport to the waterfront.

"I will never forget the interesting and caring folks I met along the way. People filled me in on points of interest in their town. Many asked me in for tea, or to rest. One family took me to a church supper; another gentleman invited me to his restaurant for dinner. One bitterly cold day a man came out with his pickup truck twice to be sure I was all right. And my appearance was not all that reassuring! I wore old, comfortable clothing and had not always shaved that morning. Also, because I can't stand to see clutter along the road, I was always carrying a sack or two of beer cans and bottles. When the sacks got too heavy I would stash them in the woods and return later in the van to pick them up.

"I met many interesting—and sometimes scary—two- and four-footed critters along the way, as well. One morning on a dead-end dirt road I heard a muffled growling. Beneath the exposed roots of a tree overhanging the river bank, a fisher cat was devouring—I couldn't tell what, maybe a rodent or a fish. Fisher cats are ferocious and combative, with long curved claws and vicious teeth. I hastily gave him a wide berth, dreading that I would have to retrace my steps in a few minutes. Fortunately, he was gone when I returned.

"Another day I came upon a large she-bear rooting around in an abandoned garden. I stood stock still, but suddenly she detected my scent and reared up on her hind legs. We stared at each other for a few long moments. Then she dropped down on all fours and ambled across the road in front of me, followed by a yearling cub that I saw for the first time. One bitter cold day, a chickadee lit on the edge of my hood, at the level of my glasses. I spoke softly to her and she stayed for a few seconds; then was gone as quickly as she had come.

"It was not until I finished walking our two southernmost counties that I realized I was the first 251 Club member ever to have walked in all the towns. On November 7, 1999, I reached my goal of having walked every road in the state of Vermont–except for the interstates, on which pedestrians are prohibited. My mileage totaled 25,000.

"I never set out to earn my "unique-plus" membership, but on the road of life it is rare to set out for the destination we eventually reach."

—By Edward A. Keenan Jr., M.D.,
as told to Ione Lacy Keenan 🍁

VERMONT'S ISLANDS IN THE SUN—AND OCCASIONALLY SNOW

Grand Isle County

The major Champlain Islands are South Hero and Grand Isle (actually one island), North Hero, and Isle la Motte. North and South Hero originally were named the Two Heroes by Ethan Allen. He bought the land after the Revolutionary War and parceled grants to a number of other Green Mountain Boys, immodestly naming them, it is said, for himself and fellow hero brother Ira. In 1798 Two Heroes was divided into North Hero, Middle Hero (later renamed Grand Isle), and South Hero.

Touring the Champlain Islands, which usually tops the "visit-during-the-summer-at-your-own-risk" list, can be similarly busy, but not overwhelmingly so. Anyway, the views are striking. Before you go, pick up a "Chamber Map and Business Guide for Vermont's Champlain Islands" from a tourist information outlet.

Before mentioning specific things and places—any of them apt to change over the life of this book's edition—contact the Lake Champlain Islands Economic Development Association. Its website is: http://www.champlainislands.com/contact-us-2/. Executive Director Sherri Potvin is on top of everything. Her office is at 3501 U.S. Route 2 in North Hero, and her phone number is 802.372.8400. She isn't there weekends, but office hours are 9-4 Monday-Wednesday and Friday. If you're in the area, drop by and let her know how long you'll be staying, and what kinds of things you and your family like to do. To get to Sherri's office in North Hero you must first drive through South Hero though, so let's begin there.

Visitors to Hero's Welcome country store and deli in North Hero arrive, it is said, by car, bike motorcycle, canoe, kayak, horse, seaplane, ferry and water skis. Walk in and you'll make history.

South Hero

Apple Island Resort - 71 Route 2, South Hero, VT 05486 www.appleislandresort.com getinfo@appleislandresort.com 802.372.3800.
Located on the southern tip of the Island, this fine RV resort features an executive golf course, marina with boat rentals, general store, hot tub, heated pool, community center and fitness room. Accommodations include campsites, cabins, and fully furnished cottage rentals.

Local Motion The Island Line Bike Ferry - One Steele Street, Burlington, VT 05401 www.localmotion.org 802.861.2700 You're your Island Line Bike Trail connection between Burlington and the Champlain Islands. Operate seasonally, check website for details.

To rent bicycles, visit trailside center directly on the bike path at Burlington waterfront.

Grand Isle

Hyde Log Cabin | Block Schoolhouse -228-230 Route 2, Grand Isle, VT 05458 - http://historicvermont.org/sites/html/hyde.html.Open Memorial Day through Columbus Day, Friday through Monday, 11 a.m.-5 p.m. 802.372.4024. Follow Route 2 east through South Hero. Jedediah Hyde Jr. fought in the Revolutionary War after enlisting in the Connecticut Grenadiers at age fourteen. Jedediah Jr. remained on Grand Isle and built a cabin there, which was home to various members of his family for 150 years. The Block Schoolhouse, built In 1814, was first used as a stockade In the War of 1814, then a church, and later a school, and finally, a place to host town meetings.

Grand Isle Lake House Go south on Route 2 across the bridge between North Hero and Grand Isle. Take a left on East Shore Road and continue 0.7 miles.; www.grandislelakehouse.com The Lake House is on the right between two stone pillars., one of the most stunning properties on the Champlain Islands, is the setting for two other events on Grand Isle. A three-story Victorian mansion framed by a 12-foot-wide wraparound porch, it rests on a narrow peninsula with unparalleled views of Lake Champlain islands and the Green Mountains. It was built as a hotel in 1903 and donated to the Preservation Trust of Vermont in 1997 after 35 years as a girls' summer camp.

Vermont Jazz Ensemble - The seventeen-member jazz ensemble makes an annual appearance at the Grand Isle Lake House each August. The group performs largely in "Big Band" style, also playing blues, Latin, rock, and fusion. The Ensemble made its first appearance at a 1976 YMCA Camp Abenaki jazz weekend and has grown con-tinually in popularity since then. If you like Glenn Miller, Duke Ellington, Count Basie, Stan Kenton, or Woody Herman, you'll love the Vermont Jazz Ensemble. See their website for a complete schedule. They have many dates elsewhere in the state. Admission; www.vermontjazzensemble.com.

North Hero

Knight Point State Park. At the southern tip of North Hero, is just off Route 2 on the north side of the bridge separating Grand Isle from North Hero. John Knight, first resident and owner of the ferry that ran between Knight Point and Grand Isle, built a home there that today is a park staff residence. Knight and his family operated the ferry from 1785 until the first bridge opened in 1892

Here's a plan on a nice day. If it's snack- or meal-time, call Sherri Potvin (see page 213), if you haven't already. Then snag a lakeside table and order at "Hero's Welcome" a country store and deli two doors away. Everything's very tasty, and you may find a souvenir you like. Now you'll have time to go through your Islands itinerary—or your brochures if you don't yet have a set schedule for the day—and begin to put one together Either way, the scenery is magnificent. (The YouTube video below the next description may help.)

Isle La Motte

Chazy Fossil Reef. Take U.S. Route 2 through North Hero to Route 129. Go left through South Alburgh across the bridge to Isle La Motte. Take a left on Main Street and go about 2 miles. Take another left on Quarry Road (the stone building on the right houses the Isle La Motte Historical Society). The Goodsell Ridge Preserve is about a half mile farther, on the left side of Quarry Road. The preserve is open dawn to dusk for self-guided tours. Call (802) 862-4150.

The last supercontinent—called Pangaea—existed from 300 or so million years ago to about 200 million years ago, when Pangaea began breaking up into the configuration of continents that exists today. When you look at this ancient landmass the first thing you notice is that the area now occupied by Vermont is sandwiched between what is now Europe and the eastern edge of North America. At that time, the Green Mountain State was almost on the equator.

You can learn more from Vermont state naturalist Charles Johnson's book, *The Nature of Vermont* (see the bibliography. You can also find out for yourself with a trip to the Goodsell Ridge Fossil Preserve. Here more than a half-dozen outcroppings in a meadow a quarter mile from the lake reveal parts of an ancient coral reef thrust to the surface from many hundreds of feet below. The remains of sponges, trilobites, and other extinct ancestors are all on display. A nearby farmhouse serves as the site's research center and museum.

YOUTUBE VIDEO:
"Vermont Spotlight - Champlain Islands" (4:54)
(A five-minute summary of the Islands' attractions) ❧

ALBURGH'S BINATIONAL CUSTOMS HOUSE

In 1781 the Vermont legislature granted to Ira Allen and sixty-four associates the only town in Grand Isle County that was not a Lake Champlain island. This was Alburgh, a peninsula connected by bridges to the other island towns. In those days smuggling was known to occur across the Canadian border, especially during Prohibition. Since then the U.S. and Canadian governments have collaborated to build a common customs house along the U.S.–Canada boundary line in Alburgh. It is the only customs house operated and maintained by both countries on the entire international border.

After you visit the Customs House, don't miss nearby Alburgh Dunes State Park, boasting the longest undeveloped natural beach on the Vermont side of Lake Champlain. There's lots to do, including swimming, picnicking, fishing and hiking. If you're interested in boating, choose from kayaks, canoes, and rowboats—all for rent, by the hour or the whole day.

YOUTUBE VIDEO:
"Alburgh Dunes State Park" (2:20)

ROBERT F. WILSON

NO PLACE FOR THE DEVIL IN THE OLD ROUND CHURCH

Richmond

Right. No corners equals no place for the Devil to hide. That's one theory, anyway, accounting for churches built in this manner. Richmond's Old Round Church doesn't really qualify, because it consists of sixteen sides, which still, of course, leaves corners, albeit pretty skimpy ones.

The Old Round Church was built in 1813 as a nondenominational meetinghouse, with the town's Baptists, Universalists, Congregationalists, and Methodists all sharing the facilities, and all serving as proprietors. The land was donated by a tavern keeper and a storekeeper, and the church construction costs came to $2,305.42—all raised by the sale of pews.

This church held up for 160 years, when it was closed by state officials as unsafe for public use. In 1976 the church was turned over to the Richmond Historical Society for restoration. Five years and $180,000 later, the church was opened again and has remained so. A second restoration now under way will add a new cedar shingle roof, sprinkler system, handrails to the balcony stairwells, and a paint job inside and out.

Directions: From I-89, take exit 11 and drive east to the center of Richmond Village on U.S. Route 2. At the four corners, turn right and take Bridge Street south. The Old Round Church is on the left, just across the Winooski River, less than 1 mile from the village. The church is open to the public during the summer and fall foliage seasons, 10:00 a.m. to 4:00 p.m. daily. For more information, including a virtual tour, visit www.oldroundchurch.com. ❧

218

THE MUSEUM THAT SUGAR BUILT

Shelburne

**Here's the scene as Arnold Graton looked on helplessly from a
second helicopter as the silo was lowered into place.**

Everything about the Shelburne Museum is grand. On its forty-five
acres are thirty-nine buildings. Twenty-five of them have been moved
there from locations up to 200 miles away. For visitors unable or
unwilling to walk the grounds, a jitney stands by to transport them
to whatever exhibits they fancy.

Shelburne Museum is the creation of Electra Havemeyer Webb,
whose father inherited the American Sugar Refinery Company
from *his* father and renamed it the Domino Sugar Company.
Henry O. Havemeyer was able to leave Electra enough money for

any collectible she coveted. (It is said that the extent of this legacy was inversely proportional to the compensation afforded Domino Sugar Company workers.) Electra's father and mother also passed on to her their own strong collecting habits. Electra knew exactly what she wanted, and from the museum's founding in 1947 until she died in 1960, she had collected some 80,000 items, including valuable impressionist art by Monet, Manet, and Degas she had chosen from her parents' collection. Today the museum is estimated to include 150,000 items.

Let's sample the curiosities. Probably most dramatic is the *Ticonderoga*, a hundred-year-old side-paddle-wheel passenger steamboat—the last to operate commercially on Lake Champlain. This National Historic Landmark was still in service and about to be scrapped when historian Ralph N. Hill's crusade to "Save the *Ti*" led him to Electra Havemeyer Webb. She bought it as an excursion boat in 1951, but when that enterprise failed, she decided to move the ship overland 2 miles to the museum, a monumental task on its own. First a basin was dug adjacent to the lake and a cradle was built in it on a slightly higher level. The 220-foot-long, 292-ton *Ticonderoga* was floated into the lower level of the basin, which was then dammed up and the water level raised. The *Ti* then floated over the cradle and the water was drained from the basin to create the first leg of a roadway. This was slow going. Workers had to continually retrieve from the stern the 300 feet of track laid to ease the *Ti* along, only to lay it again forward, in the ship's path. As a result, sixty-five days were spent moving it to a final resting place. If you spend a half hour or more aboard, though, you'll agree it was well worth the effort (especially if you remind yourself you weren't a member of the moving crew).

One building added to the collection after Electra's death is difficult to miss. The Round Barn probably will be the first building you see after entering the museum grounds. Built 50 miles away in Passumpsic, Vermont, in 1901, late in 1985 it was dismantled, plank by numbered-and-lettered plank and transported to Shelburne by a convoy of flatbed trucks.

That was the simple part. A 9,000-pound wooden silo, the core of the barn, was judged to be too fragile to make the trip by truck. An airlift was funded by grants from Pratt & Whitney and the Sikorsky companies, and on March 11, 1986, a Skycrane helicopter made the journey from Passumpsic (a village In the town of Barnet) to Shelburne—but not without a few uneasy moments on what turned out to be a windy ninety-minute trip. Arnold Graton, the New Hampshire contractor who supervised the barn move and restored the structure to museum specifications, rode shotgun in a second helicopter. As they went over Camel's Hump, Arnold noticed that because of the wind, the silo was swinging, and stretched taut straight behind the copter rather than hanging directly below. Just as they passed the peak, he was aghast to see one of the sixteen primary cables attached to the silo snap loose; then a few minutes later a second cable broke away, and then a third. Arnold's copter landed less than a minute before the silo copter, and he raced to the landing site just in time to help workers on the ground guide the 29-foot-high, 20-foot-diameter silo into place. "It got a bit dicey there toward the end," recalled Arnold by phone. "That wind was whipping over Camel's Hump."

By coincidence the Pratt & Whitney employee who suggested using a Skycrane was the barn builder's granddaughter. Bernice Quimby, a thirty-seven-year employee of United Technologies Pratt & Whitney Division, grew up less than a mile from the barn. Her carpenter grandfather, Fred "Silo" Quimby, had built three round barns. The one in Passumpsic, donated to the museum by its owners, was the last one standing.

In aggregate, the variety of exhibits in the museum's buildings will gratify the broadest of tastes. Electra's personal preferences ran to folk art, which, as she defined it, is the work of untaught men and women who made useful things—beautiful because they have both a certain directness and simplicity and relate to their surroundings. This describes most of the Shelburne's exhibits, including the quilts, art, weathervanes, textiles, furniture, tools, toys, vehicles, and glass walking sticks. To make the best use of your time, take advantage of the museum's two-day admittance with one full-price admission.

The Museum Café offers a variety of fresh and delicious menu items, using local Vermont ingredients, when available. Wraps, panini, pasta, salads, and a variety of sandwiches are served both inside and from an outdoor grill.

Directions: From I-89 north, take the South Burlington exit. Go south on U.S. Route 7 for 7 miles, to the village of Shelburne, and look for the sign on the right. The museum is open daily, 10:00 am to 5:00 pm, mid-May through October. For more information go to www.shelburnemuseum.org or call (802) 985-3346.

Shelburne Farms: Two miles from the museum, at Harbor and Bay Roads, is Shelburne Farms, built by Dr. William Steward Webb and his wife, Lila, Electra's in-laws. Today the 1889 mansion serves as a twenty-five-bedroom inn and is surrounded by a 1,000-acre farm now run by two Webb grandsons as a nonprofit organization dedicated to agricultural conservation and education. For more information visit www.shelburnefarms.org or call (802) 985-8686. ❧

VERMONT CHEESEMAKERS FESTIVAL

Shelburne

The 7th Annual Vermont Cheesemakers Festival was a smashing success—as were the first six, I'm told. If you weren't able to make it, the essentials are these: 45 cheese makers featured 150 cheeses; 80 producers of artisan food, wine, beer, and spirits competed in their respective specialties for Best of Class. The sellout crowd of 1,750 paying guests squeezed into nine rooms and tents in and about the Shelburne Farms Coach Barn without adverse incident. In short, folks were cordial, and the pileups around well-attended booths led to no ugliness. Could be that the $50.00 admission caused a few tasters to be sure they got their money's worth—but for the most part, impatience and greed were self-policed nicely.

Wine and Spirits

Several vineyards ranked high on my list, but space requirements dictated that only one be chosen. Difficult indeed, but the Shelburne Vineyard, founded and run by Ken and Gail Albert, got my vote for several reasons:

**Ken Albert, detailing some of the qualities of a
prize-winning Shelburne Vineyard wine.**

- It makes excellent cold-weather wine, as indicated by
  numerous awards.

- It uses the word "sustainable" as more than a marketing
  tool.

- It's been around for nearly two decades and has learned as
  it has grown.

- Its impact on the community is positive and lasting

So, specifically:

Quality. Best Wine in Show for Marquette wines four consecutive years in International Cold Weather Wine Competition;

frequent Gold and Double Gold medals for Marquette and other wines; and Best of Show award for its 2014 Whimsey Meadow Rosé.

Sustainability. Wine-growing consultant Mark Greenspan has written that the move toward sustainable viticulture is alive and well in the entire northeastern U.S. grape-growing area, even though the "disease pressure is tremendous." Ken Albert agrees: "You can count on one hand the number of organically certified wineries east of the Rockies. We started as an organic winery in 1998, with organic certification. Three years later I realized that virtually every disease known to grapevines had found its way to our plantings." With an assist from Cornell University, Ken now uses only fungicides and insecticides labeled as "minimum risk."

Learning Curve Mastery. Ken knew it was the little things that would count to compete with other Northeast wineries—and close in on West Coast superiority, as well. Maximizing each grape cluster's potential was one of them. "We try to be sure each cluster has its place in the sun, is not covered by leaves, and the air circulation gets to it, assuring rapid drying and minimizing mildew formation. Ken has passed on his knowledge to former employees, as well, to the extent that today three of them hold key positions in California, Vermont, and New Zealand wineries.

Community and industry impact. "When we started our first crop in 1998" said Gail, "a group of kindergartners nearby came in and each dug and planted a grape plant. When they graduated from 8th grade in 2006, they came back and harvested what they had planted." For some reason they were much more diligent in their work as kindergartners than they were as eighth graders.

"We collect notes from people who visit us, and particularly keep track of those who say they'd like to come back and help us pick grapes. . . . We also work with the refugee resettlement program in Burlington, including people who come from agricultural countries and are trying to get a leg-up here. A number of refugees arrived from Bhutan, for example, not only excelling at agricultural tasks, but with very positive attitudes. So we've been very lucky to hire some of them to help with the harvest."

Ken vows to continue pursuing excellence and learning how to best treat Minnesota hybrids, a new family of grapes that not only thrive in 30-below winters but make really interesting and quaffable wines. www.shelburnevineyards.com   802.985.8222

Cheese

Jasper Hill's Bayley Hazen Blue topped the field.

Sampling enough cheeses to make an informed decision about respective levels of goodness was not easy. I've bought my share of Cabot and Grafton Village cheeses over the years, including gifts sent both to friends and relatives in less cheese-faring locales. But it was at this festival that I discovered Jasper Hill Farm. It was difficult to miss, because market-savvy founder-owners Mateo and Andy Kehler had snagged the primo booth position—just inside the entrance tent.

Foot traffic was so sluggish, though, that in two hours I had tasted fewer than a dozen cheesemakers' varieties before returning to the Jasper Hill booth. For this reason alone, I admit my conclusion was subjective. I bought a half-pound of Bayley Hazen Blue, my favorite by far from those I had tasted. It was the last block; a booth-minder erased its availability from the chalkboard display seconds after I paid for it.

True, I could be accused, tried, and convicted of slipshod sampling. Supplemental research turned the tide, however. In a *Burlington Free Press* article, I found that Bayley Hazen Blue was named the best raw milk cheese at the World Cheese Awards in London—among 2600 entries from 33 countries. Delayed vindication! Only partial, of course, but still. . . . www.jasperhillfarm.com

YOUTUBE VIDEOS:
"Tasting Bayley Hazen at Jasper Hill Farm.mpr" (1:56)
(Others showing the making of Bayley Hazen Blue)

"Winter Grapevine Pruning" at Shelburne Vineyard" (1:55)
(Others, including a history of the winery) 🍁

"REVERENCE"—A DREAM COME TRUE, BIG TIME

South Burlington

Driving north along I-89 between exits 12 and 13, look for an unexpected sight on your right: the tails of two whales, 13 feet long, diving into a sea of grass. The inspiration for Jim Sardonis's striking 1989 sculpture was a dream. "I was standing on a beach," says Jim, "and these two whale tails came up, with the water pouring off. And I woke up thinking this would make a great sculpture. At first, I thought of a fountain setting, but it soon evolved into using the ground as an imaginary ocean surface and allowing people to get right up to it and feel the scale a little bit more. After being commissioned to create the sculpture, I went out on a couple of whale watches to observe humpbacks. It was very inspiring."

The two whales, which took Jim nine months to complete, were made from thirty-six tons of Impala black granite imported from South Africa. The two finished pieces total roughly ten tons and are anchored by stainless steel pins in a 5-foot-deep concrete foundation. Each tail consists of two pieces joined just below the flukes.

226

Sardonis's Reverence was dedicated to publicizing the devastating outcomes of Alaska's 1989 Exxon Valdez oil spill.

Because of the aggregate size and weight, Jim's studio was too small to accommodate the work. He arranged for space at Granite Imports, as well as use of their thirty-ton forklifts, overhead cranes, and a variety of diamond saws, and supervised a team of experienced granite artisans in the early stages of the process. The first step was to cut through the two 4-foot-thick blocks, using an 11-foot-diameter circular saw. Each of these cuts took several hours. In later stages Jim used his own handheld 9-inch saw along with pneumatic hammers, chisels, and grinders.

The sculpture was originally commissioned by a British metals trader who at the time lived in Randolph, Vermont. But financing fell through, and after ten years, the sculpture was sold and moved 60 miles north to be the centerpiece of the proposed Technology

Sculpture Park. Passersby that day were treated to a once-in-a-lifetime sight: two granite whales migrating north on a flatbed truck.

While Jim was working on the whale tails, which he had named *Pas de deux,* the Exxon Valdez oil spill in Alaska made headlines worldwide. Jim decided to use his work to raise people's consciousness about environmental issues. As a result, he renamed his work *Reverence* and has completed a number of sculptures in this vein, among them those of several extinct species—passenger pigeons and great auks, for example. Currently, Jim is working on a sculpture of a group of polar bears for a library in Andover, Massachusetts, intended to highlight some of the effects of global warming. Somebody out there is paying attention and doing something about it.

Directions: From I-89 exit 12, take a right at the end of the ramp, then right again at the first light. Drive 2 to 3 miles past a couple of shopping centers to the Technology Sculpture Park sign on the left. Turn left, drive halfway around the circular drive, and park. Walk across the field toward I-89. The sculpture is on the highest point of surrounding land.

For more of Jim's work visit www.sardonis.com.

YOUTUBE VIDEO
"Whale Tails, Vermont ('Reverence') by Jim Sardonis" (1:36) 🍁

Jim Sardonis' entry finishes our story. The inspiration Jim brought to his creation inspired us, as well.

We've presented as diverse a picture of our state as we could—along with a few yuks and, admittedly, going easy on its relatively few warts. I say "relatively few" thanks in good measure to our sterling three legislators: U.S. Senators Patrick Leahy and Bernie Sanders, and Congressman Peter Welch, whose dedication, legislative prowess, and respect for both the Constitution and the Bill of Rights serve every citizen well.

Thanks for reading, looking, and listening. Please let us know what you'd like to see more or less of in the next edition. –Bob Wilson, robertrfwilson@gmail.com.

BIBLIOGRAPHY

Bathory-Kitz, Dennis. *Country Stores of Vermont. Charleston, SC; Arcadia Publishing, 2013.*

Beckley, Hosea. *The History of Vermont.* Brattleboro, VT: George H. Salisbury, 1846.

Brown, Richard W. *The Last of the Hill Farms: Echoes of Vermont's Past*: Boston, MA, David R. Godine, 2017.

Bushnell, Mark (Tom Slayton, (Foreword). *Hidden History of Vermont. Charleston, SC: History Press, 2017*

Cheney, Cora, and Robert Maclean. *Vermont: The State with the Storybook Past.* Shelburne, VT: The New England Press, 1996.

Cohn, Arthur. *Lake Champlain's Sailing Canal Boats.* Basin Harbor, VT: Lake Champlain Maritime Museum, 2003.

Dodge, Bertha S. *Tales of Vermont: Ways and People.* Shelburne, VT: The New England Press, 1996.

Duffy, John J., Samuel B. Hand, and Ralph H. Orth, eds. *The Vermont Encyclopedia.* Burlington: University of Vermont Press, 2003.

Dunn, Russell. *Vermont Waterfalls.* New York, NY: Countryman Press, 2015

Golieb, Steven. *Practical Guide to Vermont's Edible Plants.* Provo, UT: Leo Lasagna, LLC, 2014.

Goodman, Lee Dana. *Vermont Saints and Sinners.* Shelburne, VT: The New England Press, 1985.

Graff, Chris. *Dateline Vermont.* North Pomfret, VT: Thistle Hill Publications, 2006.

Holman, Jordan D. Jr., and Castleton State College History Students. *Beautiful Lake Bomoseen.* Castleton, VT: Castleton State College, 1999.

Johnson, Charles W. *The Nature of Vermont: Introduction and Guide to a New England Environment.* Hanover, NH: University Press of New England, 1998.

Kavanagh, James. *Vermont Nature Set: Field Guides to Wildlife, Birds, Trees & Wildflowers of Vermont.* Dunedin, FL: Waterford Press, 2017.

Klyza, Christopher, and Stephen Trombulak. *The Story of Vermont.* Hanover, NH: University Press of New England, 1999.

Pitkin, David J. *New England Ghosts.* London, United Kingdom: Aurora Publications, 2010.

Rogak, Lisa. *Stones and Bones of New England.* Guilford, CT: Globe Pequot Press, 2004.

Sherman, Joe. *Fast Lane on a Dirt Road.* White River Junction, VT: Chelsea Green Publishing Company, 2000.

Vermont Atlas & Gazetteer, 11th ed. Yarmouth, ME: DeLorme, 2003.

Waterman, Laura, and Guy Waterman. *Forest and Crag.* Boston: Appalachian Mountain Club Books, 2003.

Wheeler, Scott. *Rumrunners and Revenuers.* Shelburne, VT: The New England Press, 2002.

APPENDIX
ORGANIZING YOUR TRAVEL TOURS

Because *Vermont . . . Who Knew?* entries are listed alphabetically in the text, we've compiled lists of them below based on direct-line travel by highway. This way, whether you're arriving from out-of-state or are already here, you can use these lists as a two-dimensional global positioning system to plot your day's travels.

As an arbitrary organizer, all routes run either from south to north or from east to west. Entries listed are within 10 miles of the respective route. Specific directions can be found at the end of each text entry. Event-driven entries tied to specific dates are Identified with an asterisk.

INTERSTATE 91 (OR THE MORE LEISURELY U.S. ROUTE 5)

Fort Dummer, First Nontribal Settlement
Brattleboro   Ch. 2

*Strolling of the Heifers
Brattleboro   Ch. 2

Latchis Hotel and Theatre
Brattleboro   Ch. 2

Saxtons River Distillery (Tasting Room)
Brattleboro   Ch 2

British Indian Yankee (Rudyard Kipling home)
Dummerston   Ch. 2

"Taste Delights" (Curtis's Barbecue)
Putney   Ch. 2

Bridge Not Far Enough
Bellows Falls   Ch. 2

Hetty Green
Bellows Falls   Ch. 2

First U.S. Canal
Bellows Falls   Ch. 2

Percussion Instruments to the Stars
Gageville   Ch. 2

Major Angas (Inn at Saxtons River)
Saxtons River   Ch. 2

Dairy Farm Resurrection (Rushton Farm)
Grafton   Ch 2

Mount Ascutney (hang gliding, hiking, picnicking)
Brownsville   Ch. 4

Longest Two-Span Covered Bridge
Windsor   Ch. 4

Birth of Vermont Nation
Windsor   Ch. 4

America's Oldest Flour Company
Norwich   Ch. 4

Montshire Science Museum
Norwich   Ch. 4

Samuel Morey Steamboat
Fairlee   Ch. 6

Fairbanks Museum and Planetarium
Saint Johnsbury   Ch. 8

Museum of Everyday Life
Glover   Ch. 8

Bread and Puppet Theater
Glover   Ch. 8

Parker Pies Co. (Restaurant)
Glover

Haskell Library & Opera House (half in U.S./Canada)
Derby Line   Ch. 8

INTERSTATE 89

Quechee Gorge/Village
Quechee   Ch. 4

Vermont Home for Wounded Birds of Prey (VINS)
Quechee   Ch. 4

Joseph Smith birthplace (mentioned in John Deere story)
Sharon   Ch. 5

The Folly
Brookfield   Ch. 6

Spiderweb Man
Williamstown   Ch. 6

Rock of Ages
Barre   Ch. 6

America's Smallest State Capital
Montpelier   Ch. 6

Morse Farm
Montpelier   Ch 6

*Ben & Jerry's Flavor Graveyard and Factory
Waterbury   Ch. 6

Old Round Church
Richmond   Ch. 9

Reverence (Whale's Tails)
South Burlington   Ch. 9

ECHO Center and Museum
Burlington   Ch. 9

*Flynn Performance Center
Burlington   Ch. 9

Perkins Museum (woolly mammoth tusk)
Burlington   Ch. 5

Hyde Log Cabin
Grand Isle   Ch. 9

Chazy Fossils
Isle La Motte   Ch. 9

U.S. ROUTE 7

Covered Bridge Museum
Bennington   Ch. 3

Grandma Moses Heist (Bennington Museum)
Bennington   Ch. 3

Robert Frost Stone House Museum
Shaftsbury   Ch. 3

Lincoln Family Home at Hildene
Manchester   Ch. 3

Wilson Castle
Proctor   Ch. 5

Marble Museum
Proctor   Ch. 5

Queen Connie (Gorilla lifting Volkswagen)
Brandon   Ch. 5

Henry Sheldon Museum
Middlebury   Ch. 7

Bread Loaf; Robert Frost Wayside Area and Trail
Ripton   Ch. 7

Horse-Drawn Garbage and Recycling Truck
Bristol   Ch. 7

Lake Champlain Maritime Museum
Ferrisburgh   Ch. 7

Rokeby Underground Railroad Museum
Ferrisburgh   Ch. 7

Shelburne Museum
Shelburne   Ch. 9

STATE ROUTE 100

Phineas Gage Incident
Cavendish   Ch. 4

President Coolidge birthplace
Plymouth Notch   Ch. 4

Ben & Jerry's Flavor Graveyard and Factory
Waterbury   Ch. 6

Trapp Family Lodge (Maria von Trapp story)
Stowe   Ch. 6

Climbing Mount Mansfield (from Long Trail story)
Stowe   Ch. 1

INDEX

A

Abenaki, 115-16, 187-89
Aiken, Sen. George D., 40-41
Alburgh, 217
Alburgh Dunes State Park, 217
Allen, Ethan, 2-3, 112, 119,
    121, 213
Angas, Major Lawrence, Lee,
    Bazley, 48-50
Appalachian trail, 3, 5
Arlington, 66, 68
Arnold, General Benedict, 119
art deco,35-36, 208-10

B

barbecue, 47-48
barn, round, 221-22
Barre, 136-39
Best bathroom, 129
Battle of Hubbardton, 119
Beckwith, Mary Lincoln
    "Peggy", 76-77
Bellows Falls, 26-31
Bellows Falls Canal, 30
Ben & Jerry's Flavor Graveyard,
    156-58
Bennington, 69-74
Bennington Museum, 69-71
Bentley, Wilson "Snowflake," 198:

billboards, 104-06
birds of prey, 95-97
Bolton, 10 (photo)
Bomoseen, 115-17
Booth, Edwin, 78
Booth, John Wilkes, 78
border disputes, 1, 2-3, 26-27,
    109-11, 111-12, 187-89
Brattleboro, 32-38
Bread & Puppet Theater, 181-84
Bread Loaf Writers' Conference,
    173-74
Bristol, 164-65
Bronson, Charles, 109
Brookfield, 140-143
Brockway Mills Gorge, 16
Brooks, William F. Jr, 171-73
bug art, 198-99
Burlington, 202-11

C

Camel's Hump, 220
Campbell, Bob, 7-8
Campbell Films, 7
Campbell, Sarah, 51
Canada, 173-74
capital, state, 146-51
carvings, Indian, 26
Castleton, 132-33

Cavendish, 83-87
Champlain Islands, 211-17
Cheese, 225-26
Chittendon, Thomas, 2
Civil War, 169-71
citizen-scientists, 21-23
Clark, Tim, 54-56
climate change, 17-20
Clinton, President Bill, 128-29
Coolidge, Calvin, 11, 91-93, 193-94
Cooperman, Patrick, 41-43
counterfeit painting, 65-68
covered bridge museum, 72-74
Craven, Jay, 189-92
Curtis's Barbeque, 31-33

D
dairy farm,43-46
dairy festival, 33-35
Declaration of Independence, the, 111
Dee Foundation, the, 59
Deere, John, 130
Derby Line, 178-80
dowsing,178
drums, 41-43
Dummerston, 38-41

E
E. L. Smith Quarry, 138-39
East Hubbardton, 119
ECHO Lake Aquarium and Science Center, 202-05
Emerald ash borer (EAB), 22-23
Essex Junction, 201-03

F
Fair Haven, 120-121
Fairbanks Museum and Planetarium, 196-99
Fairlee, 143-145
Ferrisburgh, 166-71
film-making, 7-8, 189-92

Fletcher, Jordan, 20-23
Fletcher family, 21-23
flood of 1927,10-12
Flynn Center for the Performing Arts, 208-09
Fort Dummer, 32-33
Fort Ticonderoga, 116, 119
Forte, Vince 128-29
Fossils, 123
Fourth of July, 50, 53
Franklin, Benjamin, 112
Free and Independent State of Vermont, 111-112
Freeborne, Valari, 101-103
Frost, Robert, 78-80, 173-174
Fuller, Ida May, 130
Fulton, Robert, 143-145

G
Gage, Phineas, 84-86
Gageville, 41-43
garbage148-50
global warming, 17-20
Glover, 181-87
Grafton, 43-46
Granby 187-89
Grand Isle, 213-215
Grandma Moses, 69-71
Grandpa's Knob, 132-33
Graniteville, 138-39
Graton, Arnold, 219-21
Great Lakes,206-208
Green, Hetty, 28-30
Green family, 29-30
Green Mountain Boys, 2, 119, 121, 213
Green Mountain Cemetery, 28-30
Green Mountain Club, 4-5

H
Hall of Presidents, 128-29
hang gliding, 107-09
Hanson, Trish, 22-23
Haskell Opera House, 173-74

Headquarters for Men, 101-03
Henry Sheldon Museum, 171-73
Hildene, 75-77
Hot Air Balloon Festival, 93-94

I
Ice cream, 45-46, 156-58
Ice fishing, 80-81
Isle La Motte, 213, 216
Island Pond, 132
Irene (see tropical storm Irene)

J
Jamaica, 61
Jackson, Shirley, 74
Jasper Hill Farm, 225-26

K
Keenan, Edward, 211-13
Kelley, Sheila, 124-27
Kimble, Warren (see Henry
     Sheldon Museum)
King Arthur Flour,88-89
Kingdom County Productions,
     189-92
King George III (see border
     disputes)
Kipling, Rudyard, 38-40
Knight, Will and Terry, 158-61
Koren, Ed, 141-43
Kruger, Chris and Eileen, 14-16

L
Lake Bomoseen, 115-17
Lake Champlain, 202-208, 211
Lake Champlain Maritime
     Museum, 166-68
lake monsters, 8-9
land grant colleges, 154
Lanning, Tom, 108-09
Latchis Hotel and Theatre, 35-36
Leahy, U.S. Senator Patrick, 202,
     206-08, 228
libraries, 180

Lincoln, Peggy, 76-77
Lincoln, Robert Todd, 75-78
Long Trail, 3-6
Lyndonville, 187-89
Lyon, Matthew, 120-21

M
MacKaye, Benton, 5
Macri, Dee, 56-59
Macri, Jim and Jane, 56-59
Manchester, 75-77
Mwanukwuzi, Kikuli, 151
Martin-Wasps, 71-72
Marx, Harpo, 115-17
Massachsetts, 2, 136
McKibben, Bill, 17-20
Middlebury, 171-73
milk ,33, 43-46
Millerites, 149-50
Montpelier, 146-51
Montshire Museum of
     Science, 89-91
"Moonlight in Vermont" (song) 69
Morey, Samuel, 30, 143-45
Morrill, Justin Smith, 154
Morse, Burr and Elliott, 148-50
Mount Ascutney, 107-09
Mount Holly, 122-23
Mount Mansfield, 5-6,
Museum of Everyday Life, 184-86
museum heist,69-71

N
Naulakha, 39-40
Neill, Albert,50
Neill, Humphrey, 49-50
Nelson, Levi, 125, 127
Neshobe Island, 115-17
Neural Defect Labs, 58-59
New Hampshire,2,
     26-27,109-11,136
Newell, Graham, 193-96
New York, 2, 111-112
Nobel Prize for Literature, 86

North Hero, 213, 216
North Westminster, 41-43
Norwich, 89-91

O
O'Brien, Bess, 189-92
Old Round Church, 218
Orton, Vrest and Lyman, 105-06

P
Palmer, Patrick, 164-65
Paley, Grace, 155
Parker Pie Co., 187
Patrick, Warren, 61-63
Peacham, 189-92
percussion instruments, 41-43
Perkins Geology Museum, 123
Perkins School for the Blind, 7-8
Petroglyph, 26-27
Plymouth Notch, 91-93
Potvin, Sherri, 213
Proctor, 124-30
puppets, 175-77
Putney, 47-48

Q
Quarry, 138-39
Quebec, 136
Quechee, 13, 93-94
Quechee Gorge, 93-94

R
Revolutionary War, 119
Richmond, 218
Riehle, Ted, 106
Ripton, 17, 173-75
Robert Frost Stone House Museum,
Rock of Ages138-39.
Rockingham Township,
Rockwell, Norman, 65-68
Rokeby Museum, 169-71
Roosevelt, Teddy Jr., 116
Roth, Philip, 155
round barn, 219-21

Rushton farm, 43-46
Rutland, 130-32

S
Saint Johnsbury, 193-99
Sanders, U.S. Senator Bernie, 137,
192, 228
Sardonis, Jim, 226-28
Saxton, Frederick, 53-54
Saxtons River, 48-59
Saxtons River Distillery, 37-38
sculpture, 226-28
Shaftsbury, 78-80
Sheep, 175
Shelburne. 219-26
Shelburne Museum, 219-22
Shelburne Vineyard, 222-25
Sherburne Center, 4
Simpsons, 103-04
ski tow, 113
Slater, Ken, 99-101
slaves, 169-71
Smith, Joseph, 132
Smuggler's Notch, 5
snowboarding, 4, 5, 60-61
snowmobiles, 136-37
Social Security, 130
Solzhenitsyn, Aleksandr, 86-87
Solzhenitsyn, Ignat, 87
South Burlington, 226-28
South Hero, 213-14
sovereign nation, 1, 2, 3, 92,
111-12
Spider Web Farm, 158-61
spina bifida, 56-59
Springfield, 98-104
Springfield Telescope Makers, Inc.,
98-101
Stanstead, Quebec, 178-80
Star Trek, 138-39
steamboat, 143-145
Stowe, 151-153
Strafford, 154
Stratton Mountain, 4, 5, 60-61

Stratton Village, 60-61
Strolling of the Heifers, 33-35
Stromberg, Christian, 37-38

T
Taylor, James P., 4
Thetford, 155
350.org, 17-20
Ticonderoga (steamboat), 220
Townshend, 61-632
Trachte family, 65-68
von Trapp family, 151-53
von Trapp, Johannes, 151, 153
von Trapp, Maria Franziska,
    151-153
tropical storm Irene, 13-16
251 Club,

U
Underground railroad, 169-171

V
Vallee, Rudy, f132
Vermont,
    as sovereign nation, 2-3, 91-92
    border disputes, 2-3, 66, 89-91,
        91-92, 178
    and Civil War, 169-71
    and Revolutionary War, 119
    and World War II, 3
    most rural state, 7
    state capital, 129-39
    state song, 53
Vermont Academy, 4, 7, 48
Vermont Association of
    Snowmobile Travelers (VAST),
    136-37
Vermont Cheesemakers Festival,
    222-26
Vermont Country Stores, 104-06

Vermont Covered Bridge
    Museum,.72-74
Vermont Department of Forests,
    Parks & Recreation,
Vermont Institute of Natural
    Science, 95-97
Vermont Marble Museum, 128-30
Vermont Technical College, 46
Vermont, University of (UVM), 46
Vilas Bridge, 26-27, 110

W
Waite, Anna, 39
Walking, 3-6, 211-13
Ward, Darrell, 31
Waterbury, 156-58
weather, 9-10, 11-16, 17
weather extremes, 12, 17
Welch, U.S. Congressman
    Peter, 228
Weston, 104-06
whales, 226-28
Wilker, Al and Vance Smith,
    140-41
Williams River, 14-16
Williamstown, 158-61
Wilmington, 80-81
Wilson, Brent, 128-29
Wilson Castle, 124-27
Windham Grows, 35
wind power, 132-33
Windsor, 2, 109-12
Windsor Bridge, 109-11
wine, 222-29
Woodstock, 113
Wood, John A., 51-53
wool, 175
Woollcott, Alexander, 116-17
woolly mammoth, 122-23
World War II, 3

ABOUT THE AUTHOR

Bob Wilson was a promotion writer for *Reader's Digest*; and an editor for McGraw-Hill, Houghton Mifflin, Macmillan, and the sadly swallowed Silver Burdett. In his younger days, under the unfortunate pseudonym Pamela S. Bell, he was National Secretary for Scholastic's Teen Age Book Club, during which time he took numerous member phone calls in falsetto. He has written fourteen books.

Wilson's offer: Bring a copy of this book to his home in Saxtons River; he will sign it and also serve milk and cookies—or, with at least one day's notice, another beverage of choice.

ABOUT THE CARTOGRAPHER
AND PHOTO EDITOR

Betsy Jaeger Lawson studied art at the University of Notre Dame and West Virginia University. She has created numerous books, including one that received a grant at the Scottish Arts Council and another that was positively reviewed from Books in Scotland. She lives in West Virginia where her paintings are shown in local and regional exhibitions. Her work can be seen at betsyjaeger.com.

ABOUT THE PHOTOGRAPHER

Victoria Blewer is a Vermont photographer specializing in "alternative methods" photography, She lives in Middlebury, Vermont.

CPSIA information can be obtained
at www.ICGtesting.com
Printed in the USA
BVHW012040240721
612638BV00001B/1